Business Opportunities

Business Opportunities

By

Francis D. (Doug) Tuggle, Chad T. Berl, Seth J. Berl and Lenny Berl

Cambridge
Scholars
Publishing

Business Opportunities

By Francis D. (Doug) Tuggle, Chad T. Berl, Seth J. Berl and Lenny Berl

This book first published 2022

Cambridge Scholars Publishing

Lady Stephenson Library, Newcastle upon Tyne, NE6 2PA, UK

British Library Cataloguing in Publication Data
A catalogue record for this book is available from the British Library

ISBN (10): 1-5275-7695-7
ISBN (13): 978-1-5275-7695-7

Table of Contents

Appendix

Index

Authors

Business Management & Consultant Group (BMCG) is a Virginia corporation that assists for profit and not for profit firms to achieve their full potential. We do not promulgate a single approach to all firms and all their issues. Instead, we diagnose where the firm is today, and we jointly explore various avenues by which the firm can achieve success, as the firm defines it. Partners of BMCG instrumental in bringing this book to fruition are listed below.

Francis D. (Doug) Tuggle holds a B.S. from MIT and an M.S. and Ph.D from Carnegie Mellon University. He has written two books and 75 scientific publications. He has been a professor of business, computer science, and psychology at five different universities: University of Kansas, Rice University, American University, Chapman University, and Virginia Tech. He was dean of the business school at Rice University, American University, and Chapman University. He has worked for the Headquarters of the Pacific Missile Test Range, System Development Corporation, RAND Corporation, DuPont, and RWD Technologies. He has held Confidential, Secret, Top Secret, and Q security clearances. He has served on the boards of directors of corporations such as Texas Commerce Bank and Equus Total Return; he has served as chairman of audit committees.

Chad T. Berl earned two Bachelor of Science degrees from Virginia Tech: Business Information Technology from the Pamplin College of Business and Food Science & Technology. Chad is currently employed with IBM as a Business Transformation Consultant within IBM's Global Business Services (GBS). Chad has extensive project and consulting experience with Fortune 50 companies, small businesses, and public sector clients. Prior to IBM, Chad was a Sales Strategist with PepsiCo in their Sales Management Division. Chad's employment, government, and academic experiences provides him with the knowledge and skills necessary to carry out unlimited multifaceted projects. Chad always welcomes new opportunities and considers it a privilege to contribute to any project that he is involved with.

Seth J. Berl holds a Ph.D. in physics from the University of Virginia with research interests including ultracold and Rydberg atom physics. He earned his M.A. in physics from the University of Virginia and B.S. in electrical engineering from Old Dominion University. Seth is currently the Chief Technology Officer at GovSmart, Inc., an information technology solution provider for the federal government and its prime contractors. Previously, he founded Smartec, LLC, a high-tech consulting company. His list of technology clients include: NASA, Department of Energy's Jefferson Laboratory, DARPA, Honeywell, Northrop Grumman, and Rockwell Collins (currently Collins Aerospace). Seth is a problem solver; he utilizes his scientific and technological knowledge to innovate, expedite, and enhance outcomes.

Lenny Berl is the creator of the concept for this book. Lenny earned his B.S. degrees in Biology and Chemistry from the State University of New York at Albany, Doctor of Dental Surgery (DDS) from New York University College of Dentistry, and Doctor of Jurisprudence (JD) from Albany Law School. Lenny is an entrepreneur who is founder and owner of several businesses and healthcare ventures, including the managing partner of the Business Management and Consultant Group, LLC. He served on various boards of directors, is a published researcher, lecturer, underwriter, and presenter on many professional and industrial topics involving science, law, and business. Lenny uses his brainstorming and lifetime skills to successfully consult and promote his businesses and BMCG clients.

Preface

Overview

We hear the word or term "opportunity" or "lost opportunity" used frequently in business. The dictionary defines the word "opportunity" as,

1. an appropriate or favorable time or occasion.
2. a situation or condition favorable for attainment of a goal.
3. a good position, chance, or prospect, as for advancement or success.

What we have seen in the past, when businesses do not take advantage of opportunity or ignore opportunity, they often are severely hurt economically or go bankrupt. A case in point is Kodak. Kodak ignored the future "digital revolution," while Fuji Film and other companies were getting into the digital camera arena. Kodak felt they could rest on their laurels, betting that no one will abandon film. That was a big mistake. Kodak was a Fortune 50 company with a large patent library and decided to ignore one simple easy opportunity; expand into digital photography.

Business history point to some companies and entrepreneurs successfully find, identify, and exploit opportunities, while others bump into opportunities and don't recognize or choose to ignore them. For example, Western Union failed to recognize the potential of the telephone. Railroads ignored the opportunities offered by the aviation industry. But, Sam Walton correctly saw that consumers would be repeat customers for a business that offered the lowest prices in town. Mark Zuckerberg correctly predicted that facilitating communication with your friends would be highly successful.

So, how do we apply "opportunity" every day in your business? Regardless of the nature of your business, seeing and implementing opportunity means growth, higher revenue, and profit. In order to find, identify, and exploit opportunities, you have to pay attention. The many chapters in this book will help you consider different areas to look for potential opportunities for your firm. The many examples given in this book will help you nail down, flesh out, and implement those opportunities.

The time to act is NOW. Opportunities come, and unless you act on them quickly, those particular opportunities fade away. You need to continuously find time such that you can think and ponder your business, the actions and potential actions of competitors, your customers' current tastes and preferences and how those are likely to evolve, and any governmental or regulatory actions, domestic and internationally, that might affect your business. And of course, you need to ask yourself every day, "what opportunities are open to me today that I should consider acting on?" We have a friend, a very successful friend, who does not own a watch or look at the time. He says he doesn't need to; he says he always knows what time it is—it is NOW, it is always NOW. Don't wait; don't procrastinate, take action NOW. It is always the right time to look for and employ opportunities.

Lost opportunity can be devastating for any business. That lost opportunity might never present itself again. Your job is to find and see opportunity in order for you to take full advantage of all opportunities presented. You don't lose opportunities, you gain opportunities. You just need to know where to look. This is why you want to take this opportunity to read this opportunity guide, with its footnote and reference publications. The worst situation is when YOU don't act on an opportunity, but a close competitor does.

When we consult with clients, we analyze the industry and business of our client, while keeping all of these key questions in mind. We can then discuss a prioritized business plan with opportunities that suits the needs of our client and their personality.

We want to provide an overview of these types of opportunities that you could be taking advantage of as you read this guide. Each chapter addresses, one at a time, a wide variety of these opportunities so you can better understand how each of these opportunities play a needed and essential role for any successful business. Now is your opportunity to realize all of the opportunity around you so that you no longer leave money and opportunity on the table for others to grab.

Quotes

> "Small opportunities are often the beginning of great enterprises."
>
> – Demosthenes (Greek statesman and orator, died 322 BCE)

Wal-Mart did not begin as a multibillion dollar enterprise; it started out as a single store in Rogers, Arkansas. But, from that modest beginning, it grew into the giant it is today. The same is true of all giant enterprises—Bank of America, Facebook, Microsoft, etc. So, don't neglect to consider every opportunity you can think of, no matter how insignificant it may seem at the outset. Per Demosthenes, that tiny seed may grow into a mighty kingdom.

> "Jumping at several small opportunities may get us there more quickly than waiting for one big one to come along."
>
> –Hugh Allen (former professor at Oxford, Director of the Royal Academy of Music, and Conductor of the Royal Philharmonic Orchestra; died 1946))

Aim for singles and doubles; home run hitters strike out 70% of the time, or worse. And, per the Demosthenes quote, who knows when a small opportunity will grow into a giant one? Finally, there are many more small opportunities out there than there are giant ones. Get busy with the available small ones, and over time you will learn how to identify ones that hold greater potential for you.

> "Opportunities are like sunrises. If you wait too long, you miss them."
>
> – William Arthur Ward (American writer and former Assistant to the President, Texas Wesleyan College; died 1994)

"I'll get to it later" is NEVER a good way to treat an intriguing opportunity. Its usefulness may disappear over time; A competitor may exploit it first; costs may rise in the interim. Don't forget: it is always NOW; do it NOW.

> "Business opportunities are like buses; there's always another one coming."
>
> – Richard Branson (English business magnate, investor, author and philanthropist; founder of the Virgin Group; born 1950)

While this quote may seem to contradict the previous one from William Arthur Ward, instead Sir Richard Branson quote holds out hope for you. Especially as you begin to learn to identify opportunities, it is inevitable that you will inadvertently overlook some. You may even miss out on a large one or two. Happily, per the Brandon quote, as you will discover, there is a surfeit of opportunities out there. Don't beat yourself up over missing some—others are on their way.

> "It's through curiosity and looking at opportunities in new ways that we're always mapped out path."
>
> – Michael Dell (American businessman, investor, philanthropist, and author; founder and CEO of Dell Technologies; born 1965)

And there you have it from one of the world's richest individuals. Be curious; ask questions such as, "what if?" "What if we change X?" "What do we have to do differently to achieve Y?" "How would our customer base change if we did Z?" Look for opportunities, and once you find some, ask yourself, "how can I use this in my business?" Would investing in this opportunity likely lead to a positive benefit/cost ratio?

Ruminations About Opportunities

This book is chockablock full of a variety of opportunities (go look again at the Table of Contents). While not all of them will be immediately useful for you and your firm, over time, all of them at one time or another will prove beneficial. The authors of this book each have had opportunities presented to them, and each of us have been successful in life because we had the good sense to take advantage of them. But, you can't just sit there and wait for an opportunity to fall into your lap. If you are a passive individual, it is likely that most opportunities will pass you by. We do have some specific recommendations for you if you wish to be successful.

First, you need time to think, to plan, and in general just to ruminate about your business, your goods and services, your customers, your potential customers, your competitors, your industry, the economy, etc. If you get too tied up in "doing" (such as dealing with an unhappy customer, a quality issue, a key employee resigning, a supply chain issue, etc.) you will never break away from daily concerns to focus on your firm's future. Some managers are able to close their office door for an hour a week, not answer the phone, turn off their computer, and in general disengage from the here and now. Others need to hide in a coffee shop or a park bench. Whatever you do, you need regular time to think about your business—maybe it's an hour a week or every two weeks or once a quarter, but you need time to reflect and to ask yourself, what are the opportunities available to the firm right now that have the biggest payoff? You are not likely to figure out what you should be looking at until you have enough time to take a hands-off, 50,000-foot view of your firm. You need to dispassionately identify what's going right, what the warts are, what could be improved, and what the relevant opportunities are for your firm to advance. You can't do that between interruptions. A periodic corporate retreat of a handful of your most trusted managers and advisors is another way to get bright minds together to think about the future of your firm.

Further, out experience is that opportunities come knocking on your door, but most so with very quiet rapping. Very few opportunities pound loudly on your door. You have to listen very carefully; you need to continually ask yourself, is this an opportunity presenting itself in disguise? For example, many opportunities dress up as problems. When you solve the problem, you may think you're done with it. Sage executives ask themselves, "what can I learn from what just happened?" "How can I keep that from happening again?" Is there a market implication from that problem, or its solution?"

Another reason to take time out to ruminate on what's happening in and to your firm is to take time to look around for opportunities. Some tap so gently on your door that if you are busy attending to the set of daily problems, you're never going to hear it. Get away from the day-to-day concerns periodically and review the past to see if you have inadvertently overlooked an opportunity that was announcing itself quietly.

A Short Story

The story is told of a poor Italian peasant named Giuseppe.

Each day, Giuseppe prayed to his god, "Lord, let me please win the lottery today." But at the end of each day, Giuseppe did not win the lottery. Each day, Giuseppe prayed, and each day Giuseppe did not win the lottery. Years passed. Ultimately, Giuseppe was on his deathbed, and still prayed, "Lord, please let me win the lottery. My time is short, and I know you are a gracious, loving god."

Suddenly, the sky darkened. There was a flash of lightening and a loud clap of thunder. A deep voice from on high said, "Hey Giuseppe, meet me halfway here. Buy a ticket."

If you want success in business, you have to buy a ticket. This book is your ticket, but simply buying and holding this book will not let you win the lottery. Your chances will be much better if you take advantage of the opportunities open to you.

Finale

What are you waiting for? Read the book. Pick out two or three opportunities that are most relevant for you and your firm, and get to work. From time to time, read other chapters in the book, and explore other opportunities.

If you require assistance in either fleshing out or implementing any one of the opportunities sketched in this book, we recommend that you contact your business consultant. Please enjoy our guide, and we wish you great success.

Time To Start Your Own Business

Business Start Ups

Today, better than any other time, is a great opportunity to start your business. Why do we say this? Simple, look at all of the opportunities open to you. You can start a business from home. According to the Global Entrepreneurship Monitor Report, more than half of United States entrepreneurs operate their businesses from home.[1] In fact, it can be your home; look at Airbnb. It can be your car; by joining Uber or Lyft. You can work remotely from home as a consultant if you have a special skill that other businesses need. You can work from home, mobile, or remotely on the internet. E-commerce provides an extraordinary opportunity to start a business. Create a website, social media page, enter an e-commerce channel, and you are up and running. It's never been easier and cheaper to start a business.

According to the Webster's Dictionary, the definition of *business* is:

1. An occupation, profession, or trade.
2. The purchase and sale of goods in an attempt to make a profit.
3. A person, partnership, or corporation engaged in commerce, manufacturing, or a service; profit-seeking enterprise or concern.

One of the most asked business questions is, "When is the best time to start a business?" There are several good answers to that question. It is best to start a business when you are:

- Younger
- Unemployed
- Unhappy at your 9 to 5 job
- Free of responsibilities
- Motivated
- Acquiring that entrepreneurial urge
- Desiring to be your own boss

Bottom line, the best time to start your own business is TODAY. Seize the present and don't leave "opportunity" behind.

When considering the *timing* of starting your business, be aware of the economy and economic conditions. Is the economy strong, or is the economy weak? Join your local or regional Chamber

of Commerce, Kiwanis Club, or business network groups to meet like-minded people and make introductions. Either way, you are encouraged to start your business when YOU are ready. Believe it or not, there are advantages to starting a business in a bad economy. First, if you are working at a full-time job, the additional new business income can help if you are laid off. Second, supply and demand will work in your favor with production costs. Because of a slower economy, you should be able to negotiate better production pricing and costs. Additionally, your suppliers won't be as busy and will be able to spend more time with you to create a better product or service. Lastly, a slower economy gives you the chance to have more control of the rollout of your business. You can pay more attention to detail and take the time that you need to do things right, as opposed to feeling overwhelmed and rushed. A slower economy does cause a slower pace. So, if you choose to start your business in a slower economy, be aware that there are advantages.

You also have other options when starting a business. Will it be full-time or part-time? Some of the biggest hesitation to starting a business was the fear and thought they would have to leave their full-time job. Not true. One of the best strategies is to start a home or part-time business while you are still working your full-time job. Stay in your full-time position as long as possible, not only for the salary, but for the benefits. This arrangement will minimize risk and guarantee a pay check. There have never been greater opportunities to earn money and starting a new business.

Let's look at business *start-ups* by the numbers. When looking for opportunity, know your *statistics*. See how other businesses have performed and use these numbers as guidance, risk assessment, and general comparison. In a 2016 study, first time entrepreneurs had an 18% chance of success, second time entrepreneurs after a failure had a 20% success rate, and second time entrepreneurs after a successful venture had a 30% success rate.[2] Bear in mind, these are not discouraging numbers. If we put these numbers into the context of professional sports, a baseball player has a successful career batting average of .250; getting a hit only 25% of the time.[3] Even many major-league baseball pitchers do not have winning records; they fail more than they succeed. Even worse, professional NHL hockey players have a "shots on goal" percentage of a mere 9%. This is only taking into consideration their "shots on goal" that are saved by the goaltender and presumed to go into the goal if the goalie did not make the save. The actual goal per shot percentage is actually much lower at about 4%.[4] Another failure greater than success example is an NBA professional basketball player averaging a made basket percentage of only 46%.[5] Again, the average professional basketball player fails more than he succeeds. Even the average NFL quarterback fails 40% of the time. Only every 6 out of 10 of the quarterback's passes are completed to a receiver.[6] So, think about it, some of these professionals get paid millions for succeeding only between 4% and 30% of the time. Therefore, you can have a good shot at success as well with between 18 and 30%.

Remember, realizing that about 50% of all businesses fail in the first four years, you have a good chance of success.[2] Look at it this way, within four years, you have an equal chance of succeeding versus failing. Those are good odds when you only have to have one successful business to claim success. Moreover, the reasons for business failures are totally preventable. Don't be impulsive when starting a business and only start a business if you are competent to operate one and have enough cash flow. If you keep to these parameters and guidelines, you will have an 87% greater chance of success. Also, research your chosen business sector. Besides a supply and demand driven startup, the industries with the best startup success percentages involve: accounting, management, real estate, automobile rental and leasing, legal, and healthcare services. The startup industries with the highest failure rates are: oil and gas exploration, mining, beverage manufacturing, grocery wholesalers, and lawn and garden equipment supply stores. In other words, minimize your risk of failure by choosing your chosen industry carefully.

The Business Plan

> "Failing to plan is planning to fail."
>
> – Anonymous

Before you start a new business, write down a plan. Start a short 3-5-page *business plan* to get started. Once your plan is written, set a schedule, goals of your business, and execute. First and foremost, on your written plan, make the business legal. Making the business legal has legal and financial advantages. Once a legal entity is formed and filed with the IRS for a Tax Identification Number (TIN), you now have minimized your personal risk and gained tax deductions and potential credits. Filing a legal entity with your state and obtaining a Tax Identification Number (TIN#) can be done right on your computer or phone with your state's Secretary of State's office and IRS. For example, if you are in the state of New York, visit: www.dos.ny.gov. and https://www.irs.gov/businesses/small-businesses-self-employed/apply-for-an-employer-identification-number-ein-online

Most business plans contain at least five interrelated sections about the firm: vision, mission, objectives, strategies, and action plans. A Google search will lead to pointers to several different approaches to a business plan. Besides the aforementioned areas, some business plans look at the industry, the funding, the financial plan, seasonal factors, marketing issues, and a whole host of other topics.

We will just look at the five essential factors to get a feel for what issues you need to think deeply about. A vision looks into the future. What will this firm be like in three years? How big will it. be? How many employees will there be? What will be the size of your revenues and profits? How well will your firm be known? What will the firm be known for? How many of your customers will be repeat customers?

The mission states why your firm exists. What does your firm offer that no other does? Who are your ideal customers? In buying from you, what "promise" are you making to your customers? What are you deeply passionate about that can only be satisfied by building this business?

Your *objectives* indicate what targets you are aiming for. Your targets could be financial (sales, profits, cash flow, etc.), marketing (image, reputation, visibility, etc.), operations (hours of operations, delivery time, customer service, etc.), personal development (learning, creativity, public involvement, etc.), or a large number of other areas. Meaningful objectives must have a date by which they will be accomplished, a specific quantitative target, and their impact on the firm if the objective is realized, or the implications for the firm if the objective is not met.

Strategies are those general practices that will lead to success for your firm. For example, high quality and unique products and services may be essential for your firm. Or, low prices and speedy delivery may be cornerstones for your firm. Or, intellectual property rights to certain products and/or processes may point the way for your success. Or, careful attention to each customer's unique desires and needs may lead your firm to achieve its desired future. In general, each firm will find that a handful of general strategies are the key for it to realize its destiny.

Action plans explain who does what, when, and with what resources. For each objective you have identified, how exactly is that to be realized in practice? Who is accountable? When are results due? Is there a contingent plan? Does the "doer" have sufficient resources (money, time, space, equipment, personnel, etc.) to get the job done?

Note that the five elements to a business plan are quite strongly interconnected. Your *mission statement* should set the tone, the pace, the ultimate destination, and the set of principles by which your firm is to steer. That statement allows you to craft a vision for what the firm is to be like in the near future. Knowing that, you can then establish a set of objectives that the firm is to accomplish in the next few years to start realizing the dreams for and mission of the firm. Those statements inform what general strategies the firm is to employ so as to make progress toward the vision by achieving the objectives while doing so in a manner consistent with the mission of the firm. Finally, the action plans describe what is to be done today to start the ball rolling in the correct direction.

A good way to get started is to set your sights on your *grand opening* date goal. Technology is playing a major role with the ease of starting a new business. It is the true information age; embrace it. What is meant by the information age? With a computer, you can look anything up on your computer or smartphone, and you can accomplish most of your business startup tasks remotely all in one place. This can be done on your computer and without traveling. Register your business, apply for permits and licenses, open bank accounts, start a merchant account with a credit card company for payment, etc. Technology provides cheap storage and analytics with the cloud. Business technology can now outsource HR, making employee payroll and benefits cheaper and easier. Technology allows you to create most prototypes yourself, saving thousands of dollars. Your $25,000 per year assistant is now your $400 smartphone. Technology provides free or low-cost apps to perform many tasks for you. Technology will also better target your buying audience and improve the customer service experience. This is all much simpler today than ever before.

Think before you act. Before you form an entity or make anything official think about your business options. Ask yourself many questions.[7]

- What do you want to do?
- What are your skills?
- What interests you?
- Are you filling a specific need?
- Do you want this to be a full-time or part-time business?
- Do you have enough starting capital?
- Will this be your solo business, or will it involve family, a franchise or others?
- Do you have an accountant, a business consultant, a lawyer?
- Do you have a business idea or do you need to think of one?

If you need to think of one, here are some thoughts on how to come up with business ideas:

- Try to think of the next best "thing" that doesn't exist
- Think of a concept or product that solves a problem
- Try to identify some things that are being done already and you know you can do it better, less expensive, faster, etc.
- Talk to people and let them know you are starting a new business and are looking for ideas, advice, and suggestions.

Finally, do some online research. There is plenty of valuable information on the "web." Once you have settled in on some new business options, perform some market research. If others are already doing what you want to do, how many? If not, why? Investigate what and how your potential competitors are doing.

Learn the business by asking questions, looking for data, put together focus groups, etc. Get as much information about the type of business you want to enter as possible. If you have honed in on a specific business, product, or service; get feedback. Positive and negative feedback are of equal importance. Use the negative feedback to make improvements, and use the positive feedback as future testimonials. Most importantly, look for patterns in the feedback and act accordingly.

Major Takeaway

Our firm represented a startup with a variation of an existing product that would be new to the marketplace. During the business plan phase, we addressed not only the product, but services that can also be provided by the individual and company while the company was going through its startup phase to help support his new company expenses and his family. We did research for our client, showing the likelihood and reasons for success and failure, relative to the existing market research of their industry and their target market demographic. We were able to explain that in the United States, about 50% of businesses fail within the first 4 years and 9% of businesses close each year. In addition, 87% of the start-up business failures are all due to incompetence, inexperience and lack of funds. About 80% of startups invest their own money into the business, 40% are profitable in the first year, and having two owners increase the success rate of a new business. Based on our research, we were also able to share the fields with the best and worst start-up success rates. The best success rates are in the fields of: finance, insurance, and real estate. The highest start-up failure rate was in the field of information.[2]

Our client was not your typical business start-up being an apprehensive artist who previously was employed in the food and beverage industry. We sat down with the client, shared our market research, and urged optimism to seize the opportunity there is now to start the business. We explained that this set of circumstances that allows this educated risk might not arise again, soon. We also pointed out that there will be another income source from the two service ends of the business that will also be starting without the need for additional funds. The client agreed and is happy with the decision to start the business. The client now "enjoys the freedoms of owning my own business more than anything else."

References

1. Global Entrepreneurship Research Association (GERA). *GLOBAL ENTREPRENEURSHIP MONITOR REPORT*. Global Entrepreneurship Research Association (GERA), 2017–2018 (cited on page 3).

2. Matt Mansfield. *STARTUP STATISTICS – The Numbers You Need to Know*. Small Business Trends. May 2018. URL: http://smallbiztrends.com/2016/11/startup-statistics-small-business.html (cited on pages 4, 7).

3. *Major League Baseball Batting Year-by-Year Averages*. Baseball-Reference.com. URL: http://baseball-reference.com/leagues/MLB/bat.shtml (cited on page 4).

4. Chad Langager. *What Is the Average Shooting Percentage in the NHL?* SportingCharts.com. URL: http://sportingcharts.com/articles/nhl/what-is-the-average-shooting-percentage-in-the-nhl.aspx (cited on page 4).

5. *NBA League Averages*. Basketball-Reference.com. URL: http://basketball-reference.com/leagues/NBA_stats.html (cited on page 4).

6. National Football League. *Passing Stats*. NFL Next Gen Stats. URL: http://nextgenstats.nfl.com/stats/passing (cited on page 4).

7. Matthew McCreary. *The Complete, 12-Step Guide to Starting a Business*. Entrepreneur. Oct. 2017. URL: http://www.entrepreneur.com/article/297899 (cited on page 6).

II Building Customer Loyalty

Overview

According to the Merriam-Webster dictionary, *loyalty* is:

1. The state or quality of being loyal; faithfulness to commitments or obligations.
2. Faithful adherence to a sovereign, government, leader, cause, etc.
3. An example or instance of faithfulness, adherence, or the like.

There is always the opportunity to build customer loyalty. With today's customers, personalization, consistency, and delivering a distinctive and brand-defining customer experience are the keys for achieving lasting and profitable growth. "More than 80% of senior leaders say customer strategy will be one of their largest investment areas over the next three to five years."[1] Are you one of them?

Loyalty programs are useful tools that expand the brand image through increasing the customer base, deepening customer engagement, and preventing the loss of interest in the brand. A customer loyalty program should be put in place from day one; and if it wasn't, do it now. With the internet, social media, and review sites such as Yelp, TripAdvisor, Amazon , etc., customer loyalty is the lifeblood and common core essential for all businesses. Have you been to businesses with those customer loyalty cards? Well-known firms such as Best Buy, Starbucks, Panera Bread, Amazon, Visa, and Shell all have "customer reward" programs. Why? Because customer reward loyalty programs work. It is cheaper to provide services to a repeat customer than trying to acquire a new one.

What is customer loyalty?

> "Customer loyalty can be said to have occurred if people choose to use a particular shop or buy one particular product, rather than use other shops or buy products made by other companies. Customers exhibit customer loyalty when they consistently purchase a certain product or brand over an extended period of time. As an example, many customers stick to a certain travel operator due to the positive experiences they have had with their products and services."[2] "Customer loyalty is the result of consistently positive emotional experience, physical attribute-based satisfaction and perceived value of an experience, which includes the product or services."[3] So, how does a business motivate and induce customer loyalty? There are several methods to promote customer loyalty: "psychological, economic, technical/functional, contractual."[2]

Types of Customer Loyalty Programs

The "personal approach" strategy must be mandatory for any business. A business is at a distinct psychological advantage when customers enjoy returning due to great customer service and experiences and become loyal to your business. You always want people to be loyal to your product

and service because customers will return and refer. It is said that when a customer has a great experience, they will tell seven others, and this cliché was around before the internet. Today, customer experiences could go viral, or are shared on social media as reviews. Your best customers will be your loyal customers. They will sell the product or service for you through reviews and referrals. There are also other types of loyalty. "Economic loyalty" is achieved through pricing. The lower the prices the more loyalty of the customer. "Technical and functional loyalty" exists when it would be too inconvenient for a customer to change from one business to another due to the comfort and convenience factor of staying content with results and outcomes. "Contractual loyalty" binds a customer to a business by a specific agreement that prevents the customer from purchasing elsewhere.

So, where do you start? How does a business implement a customer loyalty program? Realizing that 20% of the "regular" customers of a business provide 80% of its income, it is important to keep those 20% returning and get those 80% to be loyal and return more often. This can be done with inducements implemented in the loyalty program. But, what kind of inducements?

To determine how to achieve the most successful loyalty program, analyze your customers' buying habits with respect to: annual purchase, type and frequency of purchase, customer longevity, up-sale capabilities, use of competitors, profit per purchase, payment history, customer satisfaction, and relationship improvement possibilities. Paying attention to these factors will help you to tailor your loyalty offers and lead to a more successful program. Based on customer history, now target those frequent customers and other customers who you want to make more frequent shoppers and higher spenders with an inducement that should work within a one-year cycle. If it takes too long for a customer to obtain a reward, the customer might not see the value of the program. The shorter the inducement time, the greater the rewards for the business and consumer. Just don't make the goal too high, too long, or unrealistic.

There are several customer loyalty reward program options that will induce, encourage, and drive increased: purchase volumes, payment speed, up-sales, profit, and loyalty. Results will depend upon which tactic you implement. Examples of certain tactics for business to business might include: sales representative lunch visits, seminar or event invitations, free premium service plans, emergency phone and website access, annual discounts, and event sponsorships. According to the Bond 2018 Loyalty Report, loyalty programs have continued to heavily influence member retention, spending, and advocacy. With good loyalty programs, 70% say customers are more likely to recommend brands, 77% say these programs make customers more likely to continue doing business with brands, and 63% say they spend to maximize the loyalty benefits, and "programs that establish positive emotional connections with members see 27% more of their membership increasing their spend with the brand."[4] Retail business to customer loyalty plan incentives can include a free item or discount after a certain number of purchases or visits, eligibility for weekly or monthly drawings for a prize with every purchase or visit, portion of purchase proceeds forwarded to charity, or free tickets for special events when reach certain purchase amounts within a month's timeframe.

In addition, according to the Loyalty Report of 2018, the top 5 drivers of member satisfaction include:[4]

- The loyalty program meets needs
- Enjoy participating in their loyalty program
- The benefits and rewards of the loyalty program are appealing
- Consistency with the brand expectations of the loyalty program
- The loyalty program makes the brand experience better

Based on the types of loyalty programs that you create, set a budget. Then, as the program proceeds, calculate the percentage profit increase to see if you met your goals and will need to adjust the program in any way that would further increase your profits. Ask or listen for feedback from customers in order to further modify the loyalty program. Also, assess the staff to see how they are handling the new program and if they are doing a good job of customer awareness. Customer loyalty is widely seen as a key determinant of a firm's profitability. Sometimes, the worst outcomes of programs are due to the inability of the staff to educate the customer about something new. Creating a customer loyalty program, planning, and following the correct steps should prove to be worthwhile and profitable for any business.[5]

> "We can differentiate between behavioral and attitudinal loyalty, also referred to as share-of-wallet and share-of-heart respectively. Behavioral loyalty refers to customers buying exclusively or mostly only one brand; whereas, attitudinal loyalty is all about having an emotional attachment to a brand, liking it more than others, and even loving it. These two types of loyalty are independent; for example, one can give a 100 percent share-of-wallet to a bus company that passes one's home to work but would still be deeply unhappy with that organization's service and be ready to switch as soon as a viable alternative is on offer."[2]

> "True loyalty requires both share-of-wallet and share-of-heart so that customers continue buying even when situational factors may make a repeat purchase difficult, such as stock outage or alternative providers trying to persuade customers to switch using promotional offers. However, attitudinal loyalty in itself is not a guarantee of profitability, and firms need to be efficient in translating these attitudes and loyalty intentions into actual loyalty behaviors."[2]

This includes:

- "Increased share-of-wallet such as encouraging a customer to buy more from a brand and less from its competitors which results in selling more units to a customer
- Up-selling to higher level products; meaning selling more expensive, higher value products, which results in the higher revenue from the customer for a constant number of products sold

- Cross-selling of products the customers currently does not buy. This means in addition to the products a customer already buys and a company that sells different products to that customer
- Referrals such as customers giving positive word-of-mouth and recommendations to buy the firm's products to friends and associates that lead to sales"[2]

> "Many Apple customers show absolute loyalty to Apple and even dislike competing products. Apple fans identify with its trendy brand and love its integrated and smart solutions, sleek design, and excellent product quality. These customers seem to increasingly live in an 'Apple-world' where they tightly integrate the use of several Apple products (MacBook, iPod, iPhone and iPad). They frequently download and buy software, apps, songs, and e-books from Apple's Store and iTunes. These customers have a deeply held commitment to re-buy and re-patronize Apple products and services consistently in the future; against all odds and at all costs despite strong marketing efforts of competitors."[6]

Consider to whom you are loyal. Surely, you will answer family and friends. Why? Because of the emotional bond you have with them. Your family and friends can do things you may not like, but you stay loyal because of that bond. The same applies to customer loyalty. To prompt customer loyalty you must build an emotional bond with your customers. To build loyalty, customer experience management blends the physical, emotional, and value elements of an experience into one cohesive experience. Always remember, retaining customers is less expensive than acquiring new ones; and, customer experience management is the most cost-effective way to drive customer satisfaction, customer retention, and customer loyalty. Not only do loyal customers ensure sales, but they are also more likely to purchase additional, high-margin supplemental products and services from your business.

Loyal customers reduce costs associated with consumer education and marketing, especially when they refer others to your business.

Given the highly burdened competitive landscape today, customer experience programs are the most effective way to differentiate your organization from the competition. Customer loyalty programs engage emotional, intellectual, and spiritual customer attributes that create that loyalty bond. When customers enjoy a product or service before, during, and after its use, they will keep coming back for more. When introducing a customer loyalty program, customer experience management provides an excellent return on investment and the lowest cost customer retention and acquisition costs.

The Customer Experience

A brilliant customer loyalty program is useless if the customer otherwise has a poor experience interacting with the sale of your goods and services. Try to put yourself in the shoes of a customer and try to experience the same set of steps that a customer goes through with your enterprise. Some firms go so far as to employ *mystery shoppers* to get data on how average shoppers are treated.

First and foremost, do your goods and services perform as advertised? Are the warranties clear and concise, and does your firm honor not only the letter of the warranties, but also the spirit of the warranties? Are any known side effects or special characteristics disclosed up front?

Next, consider a physical store. How easy is it to find? Is there readily visible signage? Is there adequate parking? Is the store well lit at night? Is the entrance to the store "welcoming?" Is there a sufficient roof eave so customers can get some protection from the elements? In the case of snow or ice, is there rapid snow and ice removal?

Is the store easily reached by telephone? Are phone calls answered quickly and by a "happy and helpful" voice? What training do your employees receive about exceptional customer service?

Once inside the store, is it well-lit, are the aisles wide, and is there helpful signage? Are all customers promptly greeted and asked if they have any questions or are in need of assistance? Are there devices to assist customers who have mobility or visual issues? Are there enough check out counters, and are they adequately and competently staffed? Are customer questions promptly, courteously, correctly, and fully answered (e.g., "I can get that for you in blue, but you'll need to be patient for 10 days")? Is customer feedback solicited, reviewed seriously, and acted upon?

Consider stores that exist in cyberspace. Does the store have a clear and relevant URL? Does your website load quickly? Assess the layout, design, and functionality of each page of your website. Does your pricing of goods and service clearly identify taxes, shipping, licensing, warranty or insurance cost, and the total? Are there any special terms or conditions associate with the customer using coupons or getting reward credit? Is the customer's new reward credit balance shown? Is there a chat and/or telephonic system for the customer to ask questions or to get assistance? Do you regularly practice user acceptance testing to get feedback on how your digital user experience could be improved?

Major Takeaway

Loyalty programs must not only imply loyalty, but practice loyalty. If a business sets out to make certain promises or uses a contract to induce customer loyalty, it better fully disclose all terms, be clear, and be understandable.

> "Air Miles shoots itself in the foot. The well-known loyalty program lurched from one public relations mess to another in the latter half of 2016. A new five-year expiration rule for points had been announced late in 2011, but the company had said little about it since. No reminders about the approaching deadline had been sent to its 11 million members. But then in July, reporter Sophia Harris wrote about the impending expiration on the CBC News website. Her story went viral, and the Great Points Panic of 2016 was on. There were wait times up to two hours to get through to Air Miles on the phone. Then came confusion and distress over the ways in points could be redeemed. 'Your company is a disgrace', a collector posted on Air Miles' Facebook site."

Our firm consulted with a business that wanted to try to grow sales without making any product or branding changes. We suggested that the business try some type of giveaway to loyal customers, such as branded fabric bags, or a free product when a certain dollar purchase amount is reached. "The giveaway for growth" was a success. While our client ran the loyalty rewards program for one month, they saw their sales increase 25%. Another longer-term loyalty program was also recommended that would provide customers with a rewards card that keeps track of customer visits. For example, a customer would receive a free item after 15 purchases of $15 or more.

References

1. PricewaterhouseCoopers. *Customer Strategy | PwC's Strategy. Strategy – the Global Strategy Consulting Team at PwC*. Jan. 2009. URL: http://strategyand.pwc.com/customer-strategy (cited on page 11).
2. Financial Times. *User Innovation Definition from Financial Times Lexicon*. URL: http://lexicon.ft.com/Term?term=customer-loyalty (cited on pages 11, 13, 14).
3. Beyond Philosophy. *Customer Loyalty, Customer Loyalty Consultants, Customer Experience Consultants*. URL: http://beyondphilosophy.com/customer-experience/customer-loyalty/ (cited on page 11).
4. Bond. *The Game Is Changing*. 2018 (cited on page 13).
5. BDC. *6 Steps to Create a Customer Loyalty Program*. URL: http://bdc.ca/en/blog/pages/6-steps-create-customer-loyalty-program.aspx (cited on page 13).
6. Richard L Oliver. *Satisfaction: A Behavioural Perspective on the Consumer*. New York: McGraw Hill, 1997 (cited on page 14).

III Setting Prices Correctly

Introduction

According to the Merriam-Webster dictionary, *price* is:

1. The sum or amount of money or its equivalent for which anything is bought, sold, or offered for sale.
2. A sum offered for the capture of a person alive or dead.
3. The sum of money, or other consideration, for which a person's support, consent, etc., may be obtained, especially in cases involving sacrifice of integrity.

Raise Prices?

A common question asked in the business world is, should we raise prices? Every day, every business contemplates price increases. However, often, their decision is wrong not to raise prices. Why? Because most businesses think that if they raise prices, they will lose customers. However, is that thinking correct? Maybe yes and maybe no. Interestingly, most businesses don't have reverse thinking and intuition that might not allow for the reverse thought process of raising prices and gaining customers. This thought of higher prices is counterintuitive to most, but well worth considering. "For example, one retailer's reputation as an upscale discounter, built through its store and product design, has given consumers the perception that it charges a price premium, when in fact its prices run slightly lower than the average in the two cities. Its pricing strategy does not mesh with its overall proposition to customers, with the result that the retailer does not get the pricing credit it deserves. One option for the retailer would be to raise its prices slightly, since customers have already baked the (incorrectly) perceived premium into their shopping decisions."[1]

Shockingly, business graduate students have no idea how to price a good or service. It is important, when pricing products and services, to consider value, in particular, what value the

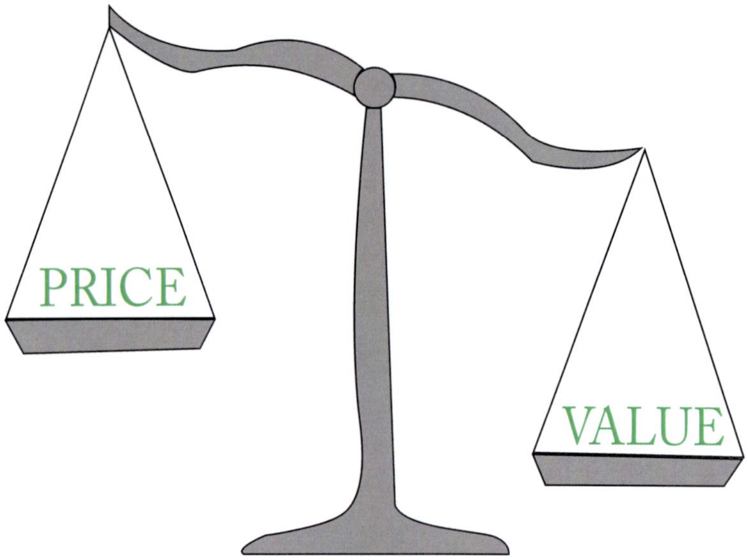

customer puts on your good or service. Try to identify the actual values and perceived values of the products and services that are being sold. Value is defined as:

1. "Relative worth, merit, or importance: 'the value of a college education; the value of a queen in chess,'
2. Monetary or material worth, as in commerce or trade: 'This piece of land has greatly increased in value,' or,
3. The worth of something in terms of the amount of other things for which it can be exchanged or in terms of some medium of exchange."[2]

Perceived value is defined as: "The valuation of a good or service according to how much consumers are willing to pay for it, rather than upon its production and delivery costs. Using a perceived value pricing technique might be somewhat arbitrary, but it can greatly assist in the effective marketing of a product since it sets product pricing in line with its perceived value by potential buyers."[3]

As you can see, perceived value provides an opportunity to charge more for a product or service than normally would be charged based on the belief that consumers are willing to spend more for a certain item or service. Therefore, when considering pricing, always decide whether your item is priced based upon your routine pricing formula, or whether there are conditions or opportunities that exist that will allow for the perceived value pricing.

Value Pricing

There are some general accepted routine methods for pricing goods and services based on value. For goods, the formula known as *keystone markup* is used. The definition of Keystone markup is "gross margin that is 100 percent of the cost price or 50 percent of the sale price. Any item selling at twice the price for it was bought or produced is said to have a Keystone markup."[4]

This is the simplest form of price determination that simply doubles the wholesale cost. For example, if the wholesale cost of a widget is $2.00, the retail cost is double the wholesale cost and the item is priced $4.00. Beyond simply doubling the cost, another formula to determine mark-up for pricing is:

- Manufacturer suggested retail price
- Keystone pricing
- Multiple pricing
- Discount pricing
- Loss leader pricing
- Psychological pricing
- Below competition
- Above competition
- Decoy pricing
- Anchor pricing strategies

are all used in combination by many businesses dependent on their products' and services' perceived values, sales histories, competition, and location. Their pricing should be re-evaluated periodically and changed as warranted in order to adjust to changing conditions.

So, what do these different pricing structures mean? Manufacturer's suggested retail price (MSRP), has two interpretations, strict and lax. Strict MSRP dictates the price. For example, Apple requires their approved retailers to charge exactly the MSRP to control and not devalue their brand with discounts or confusing pricing. However, the usual way that automobiles are priced is to use lax MSRP—customers are invited and expected to make a counteroffer to the posted MSRP.

As was discussed earlier, keystone pricing is merely doubling your wholesale cost. Multiple pricing sells more than one product in the package for one price. Discount pricing is your typical sale price. Loss leader pricing lures the consumer in the store for an undervalued price with the hopes that the customer will stay longer and purchase more products at a normal profit margin. Psychological pricing is using more favorable purchasing numbers in the price that makes the customer feel better emotionally about the purchase. It's the old $33.99 odd price trick instead of charging an even $34.00. Below competition price is charging less than your competitors in the hope of attracting more customers to make up for the profit margin loss. Above competition pricing uses the "power of context" to charge higher prices than competition by providing a nicer shopping environment or experience. Anchor pricing shows the higher original price on the ticket that is crossed out while placing the sale price underneath, or place a much higher priced similar item right next to the cheaper item. This allows consumers to know the savings and feel better about making the purchase at that time before the sale disappears. Decoy pricing is when you intentionally place a certain item next to the one you truly want the customer to purchase. The customer will be attracted to the decoy that induces them to purchase the other item.

> "There's never a black and white approach to pricing, it's a moving target, and these are just a few options to consider when deciding on what will work for your business."[5]

When choosing methods and combination of methods for pricing items, take into consideration your:

- Location
- Demographic
- Supply
- Demand
- Cost
- In person and mail order customer
- Competition
- Profit

- Product
- Time of year
- Selling platform
- Legal risk management

The best approach is to charge as much as the market will bear, factoring the perceived value to the consumer in order to maximize profit. The most effective way to determine "what the market will bear" is to do some empirical testing. If you only have one sales outlet, your only choice is to play with time. For example, for three months, hold your present prices constant and determine what your sales and profits are. Then, for the next three months, increase your prices by some modest amount, such as 2% or 3%, and determine what happens to your sales revenues and your profits. Then, for 3 months go back to your original price and check again what your revenues and profits are. Finally, for the next 3 months, drop your prices by the same amount by which you increased them (e.g., 2% or 3%) and check your revenues and profits. These data should tell you what the *correct* prices are.

It is easier to conduct this empirical test if you have multiple outlets. Find two that are sufficiently far apart that they don't impinge upon one another's market—perhaps it is a northside store versus a southside store, perhaps it is a store in city X versus a store in city Y. Call one "Store A" and call the other one "Store B." Measure revenues and profits in both stores for 3 months. Then, increase the prices by a small amount (e.g., 2% or 3%) in Store A but not Store B and measure impacts. Go back to the original prices in Store A for 3 months. Finally, drop the prices by a small amount (e.g., 2% or 3%) in Store B but not Store A. Those data will give you a more accurate insight as to the *correct* pricing.

Perceived Value Pricing

Various conditions should exist for *perceived value pricing* consideration. If one or more of these conditions hold true, then perceived value pricing should be considered:[6]

- Brand recognition
- Luxury
- Uniqueness
- One-of-a-kind
- Hand-made
- Private label
- Experience
- Social status
- Celebrity or made or endorsement
- Customer need or want
- Benefits
- Warranty
- Reputation
- Trust
- Quality
- Product safety

Perceived value pricing is one retail strategy which helps sellers price their products in the marketplace. Retailers position the item to give the appearance that the product is unique. Retailers must demonstrate to their customers the higher value they are paying for and hopefully repurchase again in the near future.

In other words, pricing a product on the basis of what the customer is ready to pay for it is called perceived-value pricing. The perceived value is made up of all the elements we previously discussed. Retailers should try to enhance the perceived value in customers' minds by utilizing appropriate marketing, advertising, and promotion strategies. Because the customer is not aware of the cost to produce the product, the retailer can try to charge what the market will bear, realizing that the customer only cares about the final price and a competitor's price for the same or similar product. The retailer should make it a point to demonstrate to the customer the additional value and extra benefits of their higher priced product in order to justify the higher perceived value price and the qualities that differentiate your product from the others. This method suffers from several limitations. Sometimes, a customer may suspect that the company has exaggerated its product quality and services. Also, there is a segment of buyers who are price conscious and do not want to pay extra for a product. The benefit of using this method is only when a company offers more value than its competitor.[7]

> "Managing price perception, not just pricing structure and actual price points, thus has become a critical capability for firms in consumer markets...To determine which of these tactics to deploy, a company should first gain a deeper understanding of its current price position relative to consumers' perceptions. Checking its prices against competitors' prices on comparable items will reveal actual price gaps. Then, determining consumers' perceptions will show whether and how they see those price gaps...there is a lot more to pricing power than just adjusting prices. Directing investments to lower prices may not supercharge sales. Worse, it might backfire if consumers' perceptions don't give the company sufficient credit for its price position. More indirect tactics, such as adjusting signage and using private labels, on the other hand, may have an outsized impact on pricing perception—a proven route to profitable revenue growth."[1]

> Perceived value pricing "is most successful when products are sold based on emotions (fashion), in niche markets, in shortages (e.g. drinks at open air festival on a hot summer day), or for complementary products (e.g. printer cartridges, headsets for cell phones). Goods which are very intensely traded (e.g. oil and other commodities) are often sold using cost-plus pricing. Goods which are sold to highly sophisticated customers in large markets (e.g. automotive industry) have also in the past been sold using cost-plus pricing, but thanks to modern pricing software and pricing systems and the ability to capture and analyze market data, more and more markets are migrating towards market- or value-based pricing. Value-based pricing in its literal sense implies basing pricing on the product benefits perceived by the customer instead of on the exact cost of developing the product. For example, a painting may be priced as much more than the price of canvas and paints: the price in fact depends a lot on who the painter is. Painting prices also reflect factors such as age, cultural significance, and, most importantly, how much benefit the buyer is deriving. Owning an original Dalí or Picasso painting elevates the self-esteem of the buyer and hence elevates the perceived benefits of ownership...Pricing confidence is an essential organizational characteristic which allows teams to sell the product confidently and believing in the price worthy value of a product (Liozu et al., 2011). Therefore, it is important that companies build up pricing confidence in a team,

> showing the team a better insight, creating more value on the product, and the product is worth the price. "[8]

Retail Service Pricing

Retail service pricing is much more complicated and non-routine. There are many variable factors involved when pricing services. "...Retail service pricing is unique from the pricing of retail goods...The framework for the discussion is based on demand, cost, customer, competitive, profit, product, and legal considerations. Clearly, differences do exist. Research issues pertaining to retail services..."[9] must be noted and accounted for.

Perceived value pricing "approach puts the customer at the center of all pricing considerations. The costs incurred by the company are less important as a starting point than the value perceived by the customer as perception will govern how much a customer is willing to pay."[10]

Therefore, when pricing services, know who your competition is and their price structure for similar services, and keep in mind the perceived value pricing components and fundamentals. Because an individual performs the service, no two services will be the same. The services are unique and one-of-a-kind, deserving the perceived value pricing model based upon all those personal attributes and elements that exist in perceived value pricing." According to Rory Sutherland, one of the great mistakes of economics is that it fails to understand that "what something is, whether it's retirement or unemployment, cost is a function, not only of its amount, but also its meaning."

"Therefore, we have this huge opportunity to influence how people feel – how they perceive our (service's) value – as well as the opportunity to optimize the customer experience in such a way that the customer is delighted and we maximize our revenue."[11] When pricing services, offer them in separate and different categories of service: "basic," "plus," and "premium." Then list those categories from highest priced to lowest priced services. "...Generally, high-to-low works better. According to Lincoln Murphy, "all things being equal (and equally good), the left to right, high to low approach seems to provide a statistically significant lift every time... Pricing strategy is hard. It's also of utmost importance, so putting effort into optimizing it is well worth it."[11]

Major Takeaway

Do not raise prices too quickly or so high that could render the product too expensive and not worth the purchase. "While Apple is able to sell computers at a premium today because of its brand perception; the Lisa, introduced in 1983, failed largely as a result of its nearly $10,000 price tag."[12] With inflation, that equates to a $90,000 computer today. Would you buy a $90,000 personal computer? Of course not.

Our consulting firm advises our clients to employ the higher perceived values whenever possible. We suggest to our clients to provide a certain level of customer service and brand awareness that would always warrant a higher profit. When this strategy is not possible with certain products or locations, at that point employ a combination of the other pricing strategies to complement each other in order to help drive sales.

References

1. Sandeep Caine, Stephen Heda, and Stephen Mewborn. *How Customers Perceive a Price Is as Important as the Price Itself*. Harvard Business Review. Jan. 2017. URL: hbr.org/2017/01/how-customers-perceive-a-price-is-as-important-as-the-price-itself. (cited on pages 19, 23).
2. *Value*. Dictionary.com. URL: www.dictionary.com/browse/value (cited on page 20).
3. *What Is Perceived Value Pricing? Definition and Meaning*. BusinessDictionary.com. URL: www.businessdictionary.com/definition/perceived-value-pricing.html (cited on page 20).
4. *What Is Keystone Markup? Definition and Meaning*. BusinessDictionary.com. URL: www.businessdictionary.com/definition/keystone-markup.html (cited on page 20).
5. *9 Strategies for Profitably Pricing Your Retail Products*. Shopify Content - For Ambitious People like You. URL: www.shopify.com/retail/120028547-9-strategies-for-profitably-pricing-your-retail-products (cited on page 21).
6. *Perceived Value Pricing*. The Economic Times. Apr. 2016. URL: economictimes.indiatimes.com/p/perceived-value-pricing/articleshow/51807284.cms (cited on page 22).
7. *What Is Perceived-Value Pricing? Definition and Meaning*. Business Jargons. June 2016. URL: businessjargons.com/perceived-value-pricing.html (cited on page 23).
8. *Value-Based Pricing*. Wikipedia. July 2018. URL: en.wikipedia.org/wiki/Value-based_pricing (cited on page 24).
9. K.Douglas Hoffman, L.W. Turley, and Scott W. Kelley. "Pricing retail services". In: *Journal of Business Research* 55.12 (2002), pages 1015–1023. ISSN: 0148-2963. DOI: https://doi.org/10.1016/S0148-2963(00)00227-7. URL: http://www.sciencedirect.com/science/article/pii/S0148296300002277 (cited on page 24).
10. *Pricing Your Products and Services Based on Perceived Value*. Trade Ready. May 2017. URL: www.tradeready.ca/2013/fittskills-refresher/pricing-your-products-and-services-based-on-perceived-value/ (cited on page 24).
11. Alex Birkett et al. *How to Increase Perceived Value (and Make More Money*. CXL. Aug. 2017. URL: conversionxl.com/blog/perceived-value (cited on page 24).
12. Michael B. Sauter et al. *50 Worst Product Flops of All Time*. July 2018. URL: 247wallst.com/special-report/2017/04/14/50-worst-product-flops-of-all-time/ (cited on page 24).

IV How To Stand Out In A Crowd

Introduction

Imagine that you, the CEO of your business, go to a new town with a population of a couple of hundred thousand people. You stand at the busiest downtown intersection, maybe it's called First and Main. What do you notice? You see people walking past you, ignoring you. Now suppose it's not you, but the CEO of Apple , Amazon, or Facebook standing in the exact same spot. How long do you suppose it would be before someone recognizes that famous person, before the local new media is informed, and a large crowd gathers?

The above incident is not about you, it's really about your company. Starting out, no one has ever heard of your company, but lots of people sure do know Pepsi Cola, or Tesla, or the United Way.

Yes, it's all about popularity. Branding a business or its products and services should never be ignored. Therefore, it is never too early to create brand awareness. To solidify this point, look at all of the successful businesses. They start creating their brand awareness before they even open their doors to the public. Did you ever notice while walking or driving, the "Coming Soon" signs? How about when you are watching TV or surfing the web in August and see a movie trailer or coming attraction for a movie that is not opening till Christmas time. These are examples of brand awareness and should be started the moment that it is legal to conduct business.

What is the meaning of *brand*? According to the Merriam-Webster Dictionary, a brand is a "...kind, grade, or make, as indicated by a stamp, trademark, or the like."[1] The American Marketing Association defines brand as "a name, term, sign, symbol, or design, or a combination of them, intended to identify the goods or services of one seller or group of sellers and to differentiate them from those of competitors".[2]

So, why is having a brand or brand awareness so important? There are many good reasons. Most importantly, brand awareness is an asset that gets the business noticed and helps to sell its merchandise and services. The perfect go-to examples of brand awareness are: McDonald's, Microsoft, Apple, Coca-Cola, IBM, Nike, Intel, GE, and BMW. The public immediately recognizes their names, slogans, and their logos. Who has never seen or heard of McDonald's *Golden Arches*? You can't go anywhere in the world without noticing these brands. How does this happen? How can a name, slogan, image or logo be so recognizable around the world?

For the reasons of immediate name and brand recognition, brand awareness adds monetary value, loyalty, identity, and legal protection to a business. This is known as brand value, adding an additional monetary asset to a business, making that business much more valuable. If you are in business to make money while you own the business and at the time of its sale, branding your business is a must. A brand is a tangible business asset that has tremendous value.

Golden arches. Image sourced from Wikipedia.[3]

Develop A Brand For Your Business

A brand is created by adding a central component to your business through a *Trademark* that uniquely identifies the "good will" and "reputation" of the business through a legal trademark purchased from and filed with the United States Patent and Trademark Office (USPTO). "Having a trademark component of your business plan is critical to your success."[4] To register a trademark, go to the U.S. Patent and Trademark Office's web site at www.uspto.gov. Before you attempt to register your trademark brand, make sure someone else hasn't already registered the mark in your category by checking the Trademark Electronic Search System database. If your trademark is declined for the reason that someone else might own those rights and you believe this might be incorrect, you can call the trademark examiner to discuss your case and/or consult with a copyright and trademark attorney to look into the matter further. If after your investigation the trademark is already taken, then develop a new brand and reapply with the new trademark.

Notice, when businesses with great brands such as: Google, Nike, Apple, McDonald's, IBM and Coca-Cola portray the name of the company, their brand resonates their entire brand concept of what they are all about and connects the company with its customers and their common perspectives. Proper use of brand and a brand building process will create and maintain loyal customer relationships, generate referrals, and fend off competitor and disgruntled customer attacks. Successful companies require proper brand management and constant control over their image to maintain their status in the marketplace. It is essential for companies to have knowledge of brand building processes and a well thought out branding strategy present in their business plan in order to achieve proper brand management that results in a consistent competitive advantage over the competition.

A greater brand will then convince customers that there are significantly greater differences among the lesser brands. Brand elements or identities that contribute to creating the brand are:

- Brand names
- URLs
- Logos
- Symbols
- Characters
- Spokespeople
- Slogans
- Jingles
- Packages
- Social media
- Cause related charitable giving
- Co-branding
- Signage

Brand elements are most effective when those elements are most memorable, meaningful, likable, transferable, adaptable, and protectable. With globalization, innovation, and technology, there will be changes to these elements over time and they will have a certain defined life cycle. Note how the once omnipresent Polaroid brand disappeared.

What is the life cycle of a brand? There are four stages to the life cycle of any brand: Introduction, Growth, Maturity, and Decline. In order to promote growth and avoid decline, it is important to constantly improve the brand by always implementing new and additional features and versions of the product or service in order to generate future market segments that will affect sales growth positively, especially during mergers and acquisitions or customer demographic changes. When competition is stiff, information flow is unstoppable, and consumers have more possibilities than ever; getting the right attention for your business is a crucial part of doing business. Proper branding gets the attention the business needs to thrive. Otherwise, without a brand, or a decline in the brand, the business is more likely to fail.

Promoting Your Brand

The first step to take to promote your brand, to get it recognized by prospective consumers, is to understand your target market. In particular, you need to understand who IS a possible customer for your goods or services, and who IS NOT. Don't waste your time, energy, and finances trying to influence people who would never purchase from you. If you think your good or service should appeal to everyone, rethink. Would pensioners buy from you? How about high school students? Would the deaf or blind? Would people living at or below the poverty line? What about billionaires? Would policemen in Belgium? New-borns? Fishermen in the Philippines? Patients in hospitals or nursing homes? Housewives in Iran?

Once you have narrowed the set of people who might buy from you, you can then think about what motivates them, why would they buy your good or service, how would they use it, and how would it fit into their daily lifestyle. From those considerations, you can devise a plan for how you promote your brand. To take one important example, which media do you use to try to get potential consumers exposed to your brand?

If you are selling conventional furniture, it probably makes sense to simply use the traditional media: radio (what stations and programs does your target audience listen to), television (ditto stations and programs), newspapers (which ones and which sections do they usually read), and magazines. Will billboards, fliers, storefront signs, or business cards help promote your brand?

But if you are selling digital applications, the above alternatives are not the best ones for you to use. Instead, turn to digital media. Create and actively maintain a website; use search engine optimization so people searching for your product or service see your web page cited within the top two or three pages returned by the search engine. Produce videos showing your product or service being used, or interview customers to record their experiences with your product or service. Post those on YouTube or Vimeo or similar sites. Create podcasts for those who would rather listen than see. Get placed on Facebook, tweet about your company on Twitter, get an Instagram account, create a LinkedIn presence, and get on other social media to the extent that your time and money will permit (you will need to respond promptly to questions and feedback). While these steps are essential for digital products and services, more traditional firms would be foolish not to take such steps as well.

Protecting Your Brand

So how do you protect your brand from piracy and being counterfeited? It falls upon you to vigilantly look for fakes (Duncan Donuts, Admiral Motors, Macrosoft, Appel Computers, Facebulk, etc.). You have to vigorously prosecute those who try to steal your brand. "Brand piracy is the act of naming a product in a manner which can result in confusion with other better-known brands. According to author Robert Tönnis, the term brand piracy is unauthorized usage of protected brand names, labels, designs or description of trade".[2] Unfortunately, there are some countries that do not honor intellectual property (IP) law. Unless those individuals from those noncompliant countries step foot in the US or a compliant country, they can't be prosecuted. Two of the largest noncompliant countries are China and India. When countries don't follow US and international IP laws, we must rely on our customs agents and law enforcement to seize those products before they enter the US.[5] Imagine how many billions of dollars are lost every year by pirated and counterfeited goods that are sold in those noncompliant countries where the US companies could be doing business and earning income.

Brand is very important. If the organization is not going to take brand awareness seriously by doing the proper research, the brand will fail, and the business would have been better off "brandless." The perfect example of this point is the beer company "Coors," In this instance, Coors tried to exercise its superior beer brand into its newly launched water business. Why would any business want to confuse customers about their products? Beer is an alcohol product and water is water, not alcohol. Yet, Coors felt the consumer would buy their water using the same slogan as the beer. This was lazy and a big mistake. Coors' water business failed at the launch. Coors has advertised its beer as "cold brewed with pure rocky mountain spring water" for decades. Apparently, this water has been used to brew Coors beer since 1873. In response to a trend towards moderate alcohol consumption and significant growth in the bottled water segment, the company decided to sell spring water — its first nonalcoholic beverage since Prohibition. While the decision benefited from the company's existing bottling logistics and distribution, the Coors brand didn't help sell bottled water. Coors Rocky Mountain Sparkling Water used a similar name and label to that of Coors beer, which may have confused and even spooked consumers. Anheuser-Busch, maker of Budweiser also began criticizing Coors around that time for attributing superior quality to its mountain spring water, which Anheuser-Busch claimed was cut with water from Virginia. Coors canceled its bottled water trademark in 1997.[6]

There are many other interesting product failures that conflicted with existing popular brands. "Sometimes, brands overextend their reach, introducing products that clash with their image and target demographics. One does not need to dig too deeply to understand why Colgate, a brand associated with toothpaste, failed to make its line of frozen dinner products a success. The same can be said for Cosmopolitan's brand of yogurt, Smith & Wesson's mountain bike line, or Harley Davidson's perfume."[2] These products should never have been co-branded, but launched under a completely different company subsidiary name. Would Colgate frozen fried chicken sound tasty to you? All I would think of is brushing my teeth with my chicken with every bite. Why would you want to consume yogurt made by a weekly magazine? Every mouthful of yogurt would make me think about eating cardboard. Want to ride a gun manufacturer's bike? Do you want your kids associating harmless bicycles with dangerous guns? Does a woman want to smell like a Harley Davidson biker? Women want to smell delightful and feminine, not like the image of a rugged male biker.[7] When branding, think about how the consumer will best associate themselves with the product. When consumers identify with the product, you will have a brand winner.

If you have a brand winner, you had best protect it. Not just legally, but with proper marketing. Too many times when someone needs a tissue, they automatically state, "please hand me a Kleenex." And it is automatically understood to pass "any old tissue," Kleenex or not. The same situation holds true for the Xerox Copy Machine. In the workplace, the order is heard repeatedly, "Xerox this for me, please." Again, this issue commonly arises with hot tubs. The common expression, "let's go in the Jacuzzi" is used generically by the public referring to any brand of hot tub. Here's another one you might be familiar with, "Ouch, I just cut myself and I'm bleeding. Please get me a Band Aid." The problem is, the generic term is bandage and the brand name is Band Aid. See the issue?

The average person would think this is a compliment that your brand became so popular that it becomes the generic term. However, this is a problem for that business that spent millions developing a brand, to later get mixed up with all the other brands on the market. This is called brand dilution. It is also happening in the technology world, when the public refers to any electronic tablet as an iPad, whether it is made by Apple, their fierce competitor Samsung, or some other manufacturer. Diluted brands lose business because the consumers are not differentiating your specific brand from others. This causes consumers to not differentiate their purchase because they don't know, or don't care about what they are buying; so long as it is any tissue, copy machine, hot tub, or tablet.

> "It's one of the biggest contradictions in business. Companies spend millions to create a brand. Then, they spend millions more on marketing that can have the unintended consequence of making those names so popular that they become shorthand for similar products. It's like if people start calling station wagons Bentleys. It can diminish a brand's reputation. 'There's tension between legal departments concerned about 'genericide' and marketing departments concerned about sales,' says Michael Atkins, a Seattle trademark attorney. 'Marketing people want the brand name as widespread as possible and trademark lawyers worry ... the brand will lose all trademark significance.'"[8]

So how do you protect a brand that has become so common? Or, can you?

> "A company's biggest fear is that their brand name becomes so commonly used to describe a product that a judge rules that it's too "generic" to be a trademark. That means that any product – even inferior ones – can legally use the name. A brand usually is declared legally generic after a company sues another firm for using its name and the case goes to a federal court. Drug maker Bayer lost trademarks for the names 'aspirin' and 'heroin' this way in the 1920s. This also happened to B.F. Goodrich, which sued to protect its trademark of 'zipper' in the 1920s after the name joined the world of common nouns. Similar cases deemed 'escalator' generic in 1950, 'thermos' generic in 1963 and 'yo-yo' generic in 1965."[8]

On the other hand, other businesses that are too popular try to keep their brand with a different kind of marketing to reinforce their trademarks.

> For instance, after its Band-Aid brand name started becoming commonly used to refer to adhesive bandages, Johnson & Johnsons changed its jingle in ads from "I'm Stuck on Band-Aid" to "I'm Stuck on Band-Aid brand." Kleenex uses "Kleenex brand" instead of just "Kleenex" on its packaging and in marketing and places ads to remind people Kleenex is trademarked. The company then contacts some

> people who use Kleenex generically to refer to tissue in order to correct them. "We've worked very hard to keep 'Kleenex' from going the route of 'escalator' and 'aspirin,'" says Vicki Margolis, vice president and chief counsel, intellectual property and global marketing for Kimberly-Clark, which owns Kleenex. "If we lose the trademark, people can use it with sandpaper and call that a Kleenex... Xerox has spent millions taking out ads aimed at educating so-called "influencers" like lawyers, journalists and entertainers about its brand name. A 2003 ad said: "When you use 'Xerox' the way you use 'aspirin,' we get a headache." More recently, a 2007 ad read: "If you use 'Xerox' the way you use 'zipper,' our trademark could be left wide open."[8]

However, there are certain instances when a business wants their "brand" to become a common noun. One instance is the business Google. Google loves to hear people say "Google it". Why? Because Google knows that internet users are most likely using their Google search engine and because Google is not a manufactured product, but a service. Google also knows that even if the customer is not presently using Google, one day they will if they hear it often enough because Google is only several keystrokes away.

> "Perhaps the best example of this is Google, a company created in 1998 when Alta Vista and Yahoo.com were the top online search engines. Google, which created a formula that returned more accurate results than its competitors, became so popular that people began saying 'Google' to refer to a web search, in general. Experts say Google has benefited from its name becoming a part of the lexicon... You don't say 'Why don't I Google it' and go to Yahoo or Bing," says Jessica Litman, professor of copyright law at the University of Michigan Law School, referring to other search engines."[8]

Takeaway Lessons

To stand out from the crowd, you need to develop a brand, promote that brand, and protect that brand. Before, during, and after the branding process, keep your attorney involved in the marketing process. If you don't want to go the way of "aspirin" losing its brand in court due to common use, or Google who is happy to become a common use name, regardless of whether they maintain their brand or not, then market your brand with intellectual property law in mind. Do everything you can to market your brand to the fullest, without crossing the common use of confusion line.

One of our clients wanted to create a strong brand at the start of their business. We did a trademark and copyright search and found that the brand application would likely be approved. The trademark brand was then put into commerce, then immediately applied for with the United States Patent, Trademark, and Copyright Office. Note that it is mandatory to have your trademark in use at the time of application so that the USPTO is able to see that the mark actually exists and will be in use. During this application process, and the first time you put the mark into commerce, use the letters "TM" at the upper right corner of your new mark. Once your mark is approved then replace the "TM" with an ™at the same upper right corner demonstrating that the mark is now fully registered and acknowledged as your legal trademark in the United States. Consult with your attorney if you wish to also register the mark in other countries. If so, different countries may have different requirements, fees and laws, so be ready for added requirements and fees.

Once the mark is put into commerce with the "TM" and applied for, it's time to protect your investment and mark. A trademark is property and has value; don't let people steal it. We also made several suggestions to our client to better protect their brand for the life of the brand including "policing the brand" in commerce and through the internet, sending "cease and desist" letters to those violating your trademark, when adding new products or services use the "common thread technique" of using your existing trademark or a portion thereof to protect your brand and for immediate recognition. Then make sure all your, staff, employees, contractors and everyone who you do business with are warned in writing that you own the trademark and it is not transferable or allowed to be used without your written permission.

As our client was "policing" their brand on the internet, they did find a company violating their brand and another company disparaging their brand. Our client sent "cease and desist" letters and the violators stopped their unlawful behavior. This advice to our client helped protect their brand. However, it will never guarantee brand protection. When there is a brand or trademark dispute that ends up in court, it is for the court to decide with no guarantee of verdict in your favor. However, when you perform every action available to protect and maintain ownership of your brand, you have a much better chance of winning a dispute in court.[9]

References

1. Brand. *Merriam-Webster.com*. 2018. URL: https://www.merriam-webster.com (cited on page 29).
2. P. Kotler et al. *Marketing*. 7th edition. Pearson Education Australia/Prentice Hall, 2006 (cited on pages 29, 33).
3. Wikimedia Commons. *File:McDonald's Golden Arches.svg — Wikimedia Commons, the free media repository*. [Online; accessed 5-April-2021]. 2021. URL: https://commons.wikimedia.org/w/index.php?title=File:McDonald%27s_Golden_Arches.svg&oldid=550117000 (cited on page 30).
4. United States Patent and Trademark Office. *Trademark Basics*. Feb. 2018 (cited on page 31).
5. Ananya Bhattacharya. *India Sucks at Protecting Intellectual Property, According to a New Ranking*. Quartz. Feb. 2017. URL: qz.com/india/906776/india-sucks-at-protecting-intellectual-property-according-to-the-us-chamber-of-commerces-2017-ip-index/ (cited on page 33).
6. Thomas C. Frohlich. "The 10 Worst Product Fails of All Time". In: *Time* (Mar. 2014). URL: http://time.com/13549/the-10-worst-product-fails-of-all-time/ (cited on page 33).
7. Thomas C. Frohlich Michael B. Sauter Evan Comen and Samuel Stebbins. *50 Worst Product Flops of All Time*. July 2018. URL: https://247wallst.com/special-report/2018/07/09/50-worst-product-flops-of-all-time-3/ (cited on page 34).
8. Mae Anderson. *Apple's 'iPad' is the only tablet people know*. Associated Press. Apr. 2012 (cited on pages 34, 35).

9. Jo-Ná A. Williams. *Protect Your Brand, Oprah Style: 5 Legal Strategies She Uses (And You Should, Too)*. Entrepreneur. Apr. 2015. URL: https://www.entrepreneur.com/article/244983 (cited on page 36).

V Mobility: An Often Overlooked Opportunity

Mobility: An Often Overlooked Opportunity

Mobile

adjective

1. capable of moving or being moved readily.
2. *Digital Technology.* pertaining to or noting a cell phone, usually one with computing ability, or a portable, wireless computing device used while held in the hand, as in mobile tablet; mobile PDA; mobile app.
3. utilizing motor vehicles for ready movement.

Do you ever wish you could have more customers? Then, you started to do the research, only to find that your return on investment would not work out. The monetary investment and the risks were too high for the low reward. This chapter explains how you can achieve your goals of higher revenues and profits with minimal financial risk.

Enter the mobile business. Putting your business on wheels gives you the flexibility to go right where all your customers are. Individuals and companies that want to enter the retail market on a lower budget without the high costs of rent and overhead can now choose this mobile option. With the low risk of entry, you now have the immediate ability to travel to different locations to sell your goods and services. In addition, this new mobile business model will help entrepreneurs and newcomers enter this growing mobile business market quickly and inexpensively, while going directly to their target market.

In addition to mobile business trucks increasing revenue, they will also act as a branding tool as you travel down the road with your logo, message, website and telephone number strategically placed throughout the outside of the vehicle. Your truck is literally a no-cost traveling billboard. Examples of mobile business trucks can include: Food Truck, Hair Salon, Nail Salon, Handbags, Women Shoes, Sneakers, Coffee & Bakery, Healthcare, Massage, Dog Grooming & Veterinarian, Tools, Accountant, Car Accessories, Video Games, Electronics and Cell Phones, Computers, Candy and Ice Cream, Cigar lounge, Sport Instruction, Not for Profit Organization, Financial Services, Job Recruiter, Mobile Office and "Hotel Room", etc. The possibilities are endless. Every business can and should add this mobile component.

With the mobile business industry continuing its decade long growth phase, every business should explore the mobile option. Look for the best source that will suit your mobile business. Take into consideration the building, construction, repair, marketing, planning and technology phases of this type of project. Get an estimate from a custom truck builder who will provide a 3-step process for best results: the consultation phase; drawing, schematic and the blueprint phase; and, the construction phase. Consult with people in the mobile business who also know your business. This way all the right items, materials and products will outfit your vehicle for maximum convenience, efficiency, revenue, and profit.

As an example, let's look at the food truck industry. The food truck industry has grown substantially since 2008. As of today, the mobile food truck sector is now considered to be a top-performing segment of the food and service industry. Annual revenues from mobile food trucks in the United States have exceeded 1.2 billion dollars; which is a 12.4% increase, each year, over the past 5 years.[1] In addition, the mobile food truck industry has been forecasted to increase by another 140 million dollars by 2020.[2] Just this one food truck market segment illustrates all mobile

business growth. To demonstrate, merely 4,000 food trucks in the United States generated over $1.2 billion compared to the 615,000 restaurants that have an annual restaurant industry revenue of $766 billion.[3]

Therefore, by comparison, an average food truck annual gross is $300,000 versus the annual brick and mortar restaurant gross of $1.2 million.[1] However, taking operations and overhead into consideration, the net profits for food trucks are greater. The average brick and mortar annual restaurant profit margin is only 4%, which translates into only $48,000. The food truck model is actually more profitable due to less hours and overhead. Similarly, we can also presume that the mobile retail business truck will be more profitable than the brick and mortar retail establishments for the same reasons.

According to the American Mobile Retail Association, "36% of mobile retailers in the US hit their break-even point in under two years,"[1] as opposed to brick and mortar investments which can take 5 years or longer with a 90% failure rate. In addition, 90.5% of mobile business trucks in the US were non-employers. This means that you can start your own business and be a one-man operation (OMO). Imagine, you, the business owner, have to pay no salaries and are able to retain all earnings. According to the National Restaurant Association,

> "...consumers aged to 18 to 34 years of age were the most likely to purchase a meal from a food truck, followed by 54 percent of diners aged between 35 and 44 years. Older generations were the least likely to patronize a food truck, with only 30 percent of survey respondents aged 65 and over having visited one. However, older diners would be much more likely to visit a food truck from their favorite restaurant, with 53 percent stating they would patronize a food truck of their favorite restaurant."[4]

Again, we can presume similar projections within any mobile business retail industry.

There are approximately 100 other mobile business truck manufacturers in the United States. Of these manufacturers, 90% of them are exclusively food truck manufacturers. This leaves only approximately 10 companies nationwide that can offer other mobile business truck manufacturing services. Here is a list of some the recommended Mobile Business Truck Manufacturers:

- Build My Mobile Business
- Elhaj Custom Food Trucks

- Used Vending; a division of Breaktime Vending, Inc.
- Roaming Hunger
- Prestige Custom Food Truck Manufacturer
- Custom Concessions
- Cruising Kitchens, LLC.
- M&R Specialty Trailers and Trucks
- On The Move Inc.
- Caged Crow Fabrication
- East Coast Launch Pad
- APEX Specialty Vehicles
- Morgan Olson LLC
- Sizemore Ultimate Food Trucks Manufacturer
- Shanghai Mobile Kitchen Solutions
- Imagi-Motive
- Cool Blue Customs Food Trucks
- Experimental Food Truck Rental Inc.
- Quality Food Trailers
- Stradabella Food Trucks
- Jack of all Trades by George

When shopping for a mobile truck builder, look for teams with tremendous experience and education who are: licensed contractors for trucks, trailers and buildings; electrical engineers, physicists, computer scientists, food science technologists, business information technologists, website and app developers, finance experts, business and technology consultants, retail business owners, lawyers, and business owners. Seek out the retail mobile business company that is most equipped to build and service your mobile business needs.

In addition, very famous brick and mortar and e-commerce companies have, or will be, purchasing mobile business trucks and trailers such as: Amazon, Starbucks, and Pizza Hut. Other companies that are not yet in the retail mobile business sector include, but are not limited to: Best Buy, Etsy, Super Cuts, Buffalo Wild Wings, TGI Fridays, Plaza Azteca, H&R Block, Liberty Tax, Verizon, AT&T, Sprint, Samsung, Staples, Office Depot, Home Depot, and Apple. However, this will soon change. Mobile business will become an essential component of all retail businesses as the industries get more competitive, with customers demanding immediate gratification and convenience.

Of course, with every type of business there is government regulation. Make sure the mobile truck manufacturer you interview is licensed and permitted that meet the requirements to manufacturer mobile retail business trucks and trailers, and have a contractor's license within the jurisdiction of the manufacturer, and a business license within jurisdiction of operation.

Also, bear in mind that mobile business truck requirements can vary from city to city and state to state. Mobile business truck owners must research within their own jurisdiction how to operate in that location. In addition, the cost in order to secure necessary license and permits will vary by jurisdiction. These permit and license rules tend to fall into the following categories: product safety, fire safety, permitting, review of municipal codes, inspection requirements, duration restrictions, restricted zones, licensing and fees, insurance, and other requirements depending on the end users' operation of the mobile business truck territory. If you or your company requires assistance with these regulations or any other mobile business issue, contact your Mobile Business manufacturer, your local attorney or the Business Management & Consultant Group for assistance.

References

1. Jessica Bianchi. *Deals on Wheels: Why More Retailers Are Taking to the Streets*. Feb. 2017. URL: http://www.shopify.com/retail/mobile-business-why-more-retailers-are-taking-to-the-streets (cited on pages 41, 42).
2. *Food truck industry value United States 2014-2020*. URL: http://www.statista.com/statistics/444924/industry-value-us-food-trucks/. (cited on page 41).
3. Myrick Richard. *2015 Food Truck Industry Statistics Show Worth Of 1.2B*. Mar. 2017. URL: https://mobile-cuisine.com/trends/2015-food-truck-industry-statistics-show-worth-of-1-2b/ (cited on page 42).
4. *Food Trucks: The Wheel Deal*. National Restaurant Association. URL: www.restaurant.org/Manage-My-Restaurant/Operations/Alternative-venues/Food-trucks-the-wheel-deal (cited on page 42).

VI Hiring Talent

Introduction

According to the Merriam-Webster Dictionary, *Hire* means:

1. To engage the services of (a person or persons) for wages or other payment.
2. To engage the temporary use of at a set price; rent.

In order to determine whether to hire more personnel, you need to evaluate if the business needs more staff. Bear in mind that waiting too long to hire could adversely affect customer satisfaction and hamper growth when shorthanded. NOTE CAREFULLY: When you encounter a uniquely talented individual who would add significantly to your organization's success, it is ALWAYS the right time to hire that person. A Steve Jobs, Warren Buffet, Jeff Bezos, or Elon Musk does not come along every day. The general rule of thumb is to always hire people who are harder working, brighter, and more insightful than others on your staff, including you. "A" managers hire other "A" people. But "B" managers hire "C" people because they are insecure and/or incompetent. Don't be a "B."

If the business does need more staffing, there are choices. The business can hire the "traditional" full-time employee, or it can hire a part-timer, intern, remote employee, subcontractor, or outsource to another business depending on the business's needs.

It is sometimes more profitable and more feasible not to hire the traditional full-time employee. For example:

- If your business is seasonal, a part-timer might only be needed to pick up some slack
- You were awarded a contract for a one-time specialized service or product and you hire subcontractors to farm the work out to that facility who can handle that type of project

Full-Time or Part-Time?

One way to answer which type of employee a business should hire would be to generate a cost-benefit analysis. According to The Institute for Public Policy and Social Research at Michigan State University, benefits including health care and retirement cost employers 20 to 40 percent atop employee salaries.[1] Many times, it is better to outsource payroll and accounting tasks in order to free up your own personnel to perform your more highly profitable work. If you do not need to hire a traditional employee and choose the subcontractor or company outsource route, the business will not be responsible to fund the hire's Social Security, Worker's Compensation Insurance premiums, Medicare, or benefit contributions. These are substantial savings that could save your business over 15% of the fees paid by the business for the services.

However, in many instances, it is still better to hire full-time employees. For instance, you will not need to continually train staff on the way you, as the business owner, want things done. Full time employees will usually have a long-term commitment to you and your business, and they will have the security of a job. Your employees will be capable of accomplishing much without the need for continual direction.[2] Depending on the job or task, it could be cheaper or more expensive to hire employees or contractors. When you know that your business will need a full-time employee for specific duties day in and day out, it is better and less expensive to hire an employee for those tasks rather than an independent contractor. For example, if a business has scheduled deliveries every day within a 50-mile radius, you would want to hire your own truck driver and purchase your own truck instead of hiring private carriers. Again, it comes down to a cost-benefit analysis. When will it be less expensive, and when will the quality of goods and services be greater? Those are two of the important criteria. On the other hand, why would you want to hire a $150,000 per year software engineer when you know that you only need a software engineer's talent for a specific project that might only take two months to complete and cost the business $40,000?

When to Seek Additional Personnel

"As a business owner, one of your most important tasks is workforce management. It's your job to make sure you have the right people–and the right number of people–to keep your company running smoothly. Now let's say your business is growing and you're sensing you need to hire new employees. How can you really be sure the time is right to bring in additional staff?"[3]

Here are some helpful hints from Entrepreneur Media, Inc.:

> 1. "Your employees are working very hard–perhaps too hard–and they're letting you know—or complaining—that they have too much to do. Complaints of this nature aren't uncommon, but your task is to determine if they're legitimate. How can you do that? Try talking to your employees and asking them to

validate their concerns of being "overworked." Then look at attendance and productivity indicators to substantiate their claims. If what you find confirms their feedback, then you might decide to reorganize and restructure roles and responsibilities to better deal with the workflow. Or you could use your new knowledge as a guide to hiring additional employees.

2. Employees claim they want to take on more tasks or spend additional time on current ones—if only they had the time.
3. The growth curve for your products or services is increasing, and you identify that as a continuing trend, not just a blip on the consumer radar.
4. You see an opportunity for growth and expansion in your industry or related industries and decide that now's the time to take a calculated risk to expand. But current employees aren't available to assume additional responsibilities.
5. You determine that your employees' existing job skills and knowledge are fine for your company's current level of productivity, but to expand, you'll need either increased skills and knowledge or a new and different set of skills and knowledge.
6. Revenue is at or above target and you project it to continue; other than financially rewarding yourself and/or your employees, you wonder what to do with the increased revenue."[2]

When considering increased staffing, figure out what type of business you want. Sometimes, bigger is not better. Will the business be more successful with higher quality and lower volumes at higher purchase prices? Or are you seeking a higher volume operation? Also, it is important to gauge the growth of the business. Is the growth you are experiencing long-term or short-term growth? If you are showing long-term sustainable growth, then it is time to hire. If the growth is not sustainable, then consider temporary employees or offering overtime. Businesses should not fall into the trap of being understaffed or overstaffed. Businesses also should not grow too quickly. Walk before you run. Use a smaller business model and estimate margins to shape and perfect the day-to-day operations of the business. If the business grows too quickly, corners get cut, things fall through the cracks, and there becomes a lack of attention to detail. If the business does grow too fast where things could get out of hand, always be ready for plan B and plan C by setting up referral and outsource systems for excess customers. By planning carefully, with outsource and referral agreements in place, the business can still profit without doing the actual work and collect referral fees and profits. Finally, if you do need more employees, are you ready to hire? Is the business set up to acquire, train, purchase more equipment, and house additional staff? "You (the business) may need additional office space, equipment, and software licenses. Hiring employees is a big step for a new business. Do your homework, consider the implications, and be ready so your company can continue to be successful."[4]

Remember, time is money. Avoid delays in hiring personnel that could stunt the growth of your business. The better that you accommodate your job applicants and future talent, the quicker and more successful your hiring process will be. Be able to tailor your hiring process to the applicant pool that you are looking for and understand today's job market from employer and employee perspectives. The more knowledge that you have, the better you are able to beat your competition at acquiring better talent.

Data

As a business owner who is considering hiring personnel, here are statistics and information to be aware of while hiring in order to expedite the hiring process, save money, enhance growth, and increase profits. These data are current as of 2018:

Hiring Industries:

- Top hiring industries are architecture & engineering, IT & telecom, and professional firms
- Talent is in high demand for software engineers, data scientists, and front-end developers
- 61% more firms are hiring in 2018 to support growth, acquire skills, and to replace staff
- The number of United States online job seekers has doubled since 2005
- 62% of businesses will use data analytic tools to help search for new hires
- 47% of small businesses cannot fill positions with qualified applicants
- 50% of employees are considering a job change

Application Preference by Candidates:

- Candidates don't want invest more than 20 minutes to complete a job application
- 76% of job seekers find a business more trustworthy when the business is actively on and communicating via social media

Online versus Offline Recruitment:

- Over 50% of job seekers apply online
- 42% of businesses advertise digitally and 38% advertise using print media to find staff

Why a Mobile Friendly Interface is so Important:

- 89% of job seekers believed a mobile device was an important tool for the job search.
- 45% of job seekers said they used their mobile devices to search for jobs at least once a day.
- 41% of US employers plan to use text messages to schedule job interviews

New Employee Average Hire:

- $4000 is spent on average to hire a new employee
- It takes an average of 23 days to hire an applicant and 52 days to fill a staff position
- Average employee tenure is 8 years with an annual employee turnover rate of 19%

Why Internal (employee) and External (recruitment agency) Referrals are so Important:

- 73% of businesses use their own employees as referral sources to find staff than all other sources
- 71% of businesses get referrals from job sites to find staff

- 51% of employee referrals involve recruitment agencies to find staff

Importance of Recruitment Process:

- 80% of candidates would choose a job based on interviewer personal characteristics

The Top Hiring Sources are:

- 27% career sites
- 19% job boards
- 16% referrals
- 15% internal
- 5% agency

Businesses List Job Openings on:

- Their websites
- Job boards
- Job search engines
  - www.Indeed.com
  - www.Monster.com
  - www.GlassDoor.com
  - www.ZipRecruiter.com
- LinkedIn
- Newspapers
- Social networking sites

Job Seekers Look to Find Jobs by:

- 79% use social media in their job search
  - 87% of recruiters use LinkedIn, 43% Facebook, and 22% Twitter to check candidate credentials
- 77% company websites
- 71% referrals
- 68% personal network
- 58% on-line job sites
- 57% publications (print & digital)
- 55% web search
- 47% professional network
- 41% alumni organizations
- 30% news media

Most Important Considerations of Employment Candidates are:

- Salary
- Total benefits package
- Employee ratings
- Contact information of hiring manager
- Work-life balance
- Advancement opportunities
- Photos and videos of the work environment

- Training and continuing education
- Descriptions of team structures and hierarchies
- Collaborative environment
- Company culture and ethics
- Number of people who have applied

Job Seeker Detailed Preference:

- 61% of job seekers say they would leave their job for health insurance
- 92 percent would consider leaving their current jobs if offered another role with a company that had an excellent corporate reputation.
- 53% of employees would leave for more paid vacation
- 51% of employees would change jobs for a retirement plan with a pension
- 48% of employees would leave for more paid leave
- 90% prefer to work for a company that embraces transparency

Diversity Performance:

- Gender diverse companies are 15% more likely to have financial performance above the industry mean
- Companies with the highest level of ethnical diversity will bring in 15 times more sales revenue than companies with the lowest level of racial diversity Why Some Candidates Decline an Offer:
- 50% of job offers are declined because another position was already accepted
- Culture
- Location
- Negative brand reputation
    - 11% of candidates would decline a job offer from an employer with a negative reputation †

Major Takeaways

Screen and hire quality employees. When businesses hire employees, certain *pre-employment screening* measures must be implemented for certain positions. If a job involves driving, flying,

† Data gathered from the following sources:

Doyle, Alison. "Guide to How Companies Recruit Employees." The Balance Careers, The Balance Careers, www.thebalancecareers.com/how-do-companies-recruit-employees-2062874.

Kanapi, Henry. "15 Recruiting Statistics That You Should Know." Fit Small Business, 26 Feb. 2018, fitsmallbusiness.com/recruiting-statistics/.

Say, My. "Traditional Recruiting Isn't Enough: How AI Is Changing The Rules In The Human Capital Market." Forbes, Forbes Magazine, 9 Feb. 2018, www.forbes.com/sites/groupthink/2018/02/09/traditional-recruiting-isnt-enough-how-ai-is-changing-the-rules-in-the-human-capital-market/.

Slater, Ben. "17 Crucial Recruiting Statistics for 2016." Beamery, 2016, beamery.com/blog/recruiting-statistics-2016.

"Top 99+ Recruiting and Hiring Statistics HR Pros Must Know in 2018." Resume Builder Online: Your Resume Ready in 5 Minutes!, Zety, zety.com/blog/hr-statistics.

Walker, Kevin. "Report: Employer Outlook 2018." Indeed Blog, 22 Nov. 2017, blog.indeed.com/2017/11/27/employer-outlook-2018-survey/

securing the safety of others, or operating heavy equipment, drug and alcohol testing must be performed. Random bi-weekly or monthly tests should be performed thereafter to avoid costly disasters.

In 1989, an Exxon oil tanker was on its way to California when it hit a Prince William Sound reef off the coast of Alaska doing $4.4 billion in environmental damage. The tanker spilled 760,000 barrels of oil into the water off the Alaska coastline. Its captain "was accused of being drunk at the time of the accident and convicted of negligent discharge of oil."[5]

BMCG was hired by a business that wanted to repackage, rebrand, and upmarket their business. We spent the time helping to develop new products with redesigned interior decorations and logo for their upmarket relaunch. We did all the appropriate marketing and had a grand reopening. Throughout the rebranding process, and before the reopening, we advised our client to hire more staff. They said that they would; however, they did not. The grand reopening was a big hit. Unfortunately, the following days, their business was crowded with customers and very understaffed. The owners did not hire more staff as planned and received some disappointing social media reviews for lack of customer service.

Do not make this same mistake. Personnel are your most valuable asset, especially when you are investing into your brand. Employer branding has significant impact on hiring talent. Here are some statistics regarding brand impact and competitor brand investment:

- 69% of applicants will apply for employment based on the business brand
- 84% of employees would leave their current position, if offered a job with a better business brand reputation
- 69% of job seekers are likely to apply to a job if the employer actively manages its brand
- Organizations that invest in employer branding are 3x more likely to make a quality hire
- 59% of employers are investing more in their brand to attract applicants
- 50% of candidates say they wouldn't work for a company with a bad reputation - even for a pay increase.

Make sure you are not understaffed and hire talented employees to maintain your good brand and to keep your customers happy and always coming back. In addition, these are the best channels to build an employer brand: Indeed, Monster, Glassdoor, ZipRecruiter, a company's career site, LinkedIn, a third-party website or job board, Facebook, Campus Recruiting.

There are highly talented individuals out there who could make your organization incredibly successful. Look for them continually, woo them when you find them, and keep them happy on the job. Don't lose your talent—stay out of their way and pay careful attention to their ideas.

References

1. Dale L. Belman and Richard Block. "The Social and Economic Costs of Employee Misclassification in Michigan". In: *The Institute for Public Policy and Social Research at Michigan State University* (2009), page 11. URL: www.ippsr.msu.edu (cited on page 48).
2. Laura Sherman. *The Pros and Cons of Hiring: Employee vs. Independent Contractor*. URL: https://smallbusiness.yahoo.com/advisor/the-pros-and-cons-of-hiring--employee-vs--independent-contractor-203736904.html (cited on pages 48, 49).
3. Javitch David G. *When and How–to Hire Additional Employees*. Dec. 2005. URL: www.entrepreneur.com/article/81244 (cited on page 48).

4. Erik Sherman. *8 Questions to Ask Before You Hire More Employees*. July 2013. URL: www.inc.com/erik-sherman/8-questions-to-ask-before-you-hire-more-employees.html (cited on page 49).

5. Leah Goldman. *The 25 Worst Mistakes In History*. Apr. 2011. URL: www.businessinsider.com/worst-mistakes-in-history-2011-4 (cited on page 53).

VII

Time To Increase Salaries Or Benefits?

Overview

According to the Merriam-Webster Dictionary, *salary* is defined as:

1. A fixed compensation periodically paid to a person for regular work or services.

Benefit is defined as:

1. Something that is advantageous or good; an advantage.
2. A payment or gift, as one made to help someone or given by an employer, an insurance company, or a public agency.
3. Theatrical performance or other public entertainment to raise money for a charitable organization or cause.

Here is a good question. If you own a business, or you are in charge of the bottom line, you resist salary and benefit increases as long as possible. On the other hand, if you are a talent recruiter, in human resources, or manage a department; you want the best talent money could buy. These departments are not concerned with escalating employment costs. As you can see, there can be competing interests within the same company. Underpaying staff can lead to low morale and high turnover. Overpayment can lead to less profit and slowed business growth, so where is the happy medium? How do you strike a balance? How do you make sure you are not overpaying or underpaying for staff? Are there guidelines?

Factors to Consider

When considering salary and benefit compensation, know the world around you. Is unemployment high or low? How many workers and with what skills are sitting on the sideline out of the workforce? For good or bad, businesses and workforces are global. Businesses and people will "go where the money is." Certain businesses will determine locations based on the lower cost of workforce. Workforce cost is a major component of the business formula. In addition, workers will migrate to higher wage areas. When calculating salaries and benefits, it is essential to "know the world around you." Just as companies travel to low cost wage areas, people travel to high cost wage areas. It is a constant dynamic, battle, and competition for money.

Another factor to consider is the cost of living of your business location. Employees are willing to tolerate lower wages and benefits, knowing they will reside in an area with a lower cost of living that offsets the higher wage. Therefore, if your business is in a lower cost of living area, you can get away with paying lower salaries and benefits. According to U.S. News & World Report , the 10 lowest cost of living urban areas in the U.S. in 2018 are as follows:[1]

10. Buffalo, New York

9. Minneapolis-St. Paul, Minnesota

8. Fayetteville, Arkansas

7. Omaha, Nebraska
6. Salt Lake City, Utah
5. Indianapolis, Indiana
4. Grand Rapids, Michigan
3. Des Moines, Iowa
2. Fort Wayne, Indiana
1. Huntsville, Alabama

In addition, according to CNBC , the top 10 US cities in 2018 with high-paying jobs and low cost of living include:[2]

10. Charlotte, North Carolina
9. Dallas, Texas
8. Tampa, Florida
7. Bakersfield, California
6. Omaha, Nebraska
5. Durham, North Carolina
4. Phoenix, Arizona
3. Lexington, Kentucky
2. Kansas City, Missouri
1. Oklahoma City, Oklahoma

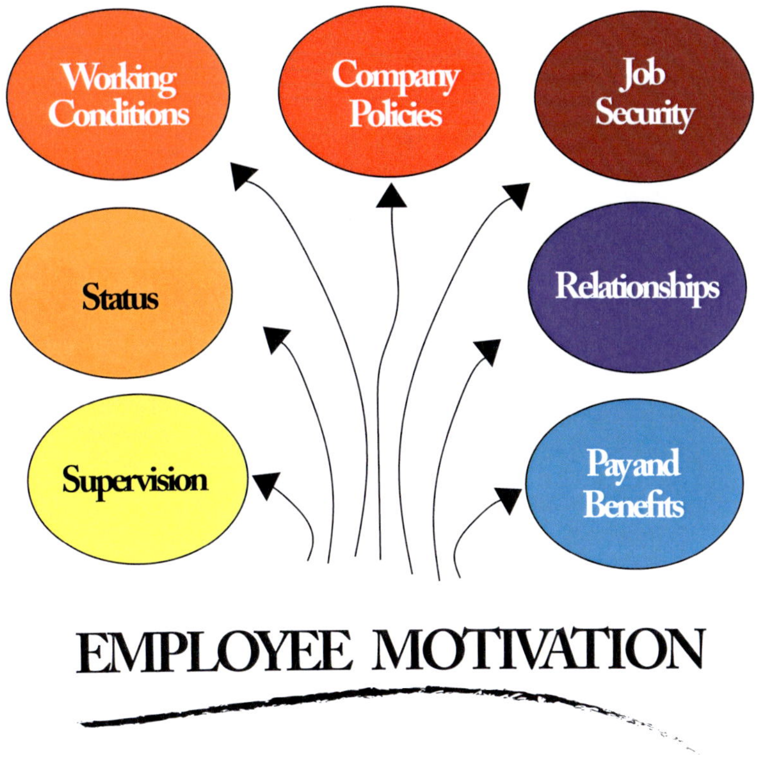

Now, we are not suggesting that every employee and business run to the highest salary and lowest cost of business area, respectively. However, what we are suggesting is that you know all the variables surrounding your business, to make a wise payroll decision and be able to justify salaries and benefits to your employees. Several of the best sites to research salaries and reviews made by employers, taking into consideration of all these variables and in real time, include Indeed.com, Monster.com, Glassdoor.com, and JobVite.com. These are not only great sites to gauge the competitiveness of the salaries and benefits provided, but great sites to list your job openings.

Now that you understand the basis of salary and benefit compensations, your business can get more personalized with employee compensation based on your isolated business model and success. Take into consideration: recruitment and retention of talent, improving employee satisfaction, and improving the business brand when deciding on salary and benefit increases. Bottom-line, when your business is doing well, you should compensate your employees accordingly in order to promote continued great work. You are positively reinforcing your workforce. On the other hand, if your business is not achieving your expectations, throwing more good money after bad might not be the answer. Instead of raising salaries and benefits and hope for better results, it would be best to have a staff meeting to see where the problems exist and maybe offer an additional commission or bonus inducement to test if higher pay is the solution, or it might be time to replace some employees.

Information sourced from Jobvite.[3]

What Employees Think

The Job Seeker National Study is a great resource to help the employer understand what is going on in the minds of current employees nationwide. Here are some statistics.

A new annual study is done every year. When determining salary and salary increases, what is the goal? Is it to "draw in top talent before it's too late and they're working for somebody else?" Is it to make your employees more focused on the job and less stressed about personal finances? "The best way to help your employees manage their financial stress is to help them make ends meet. It will improve their productivity and satisfaction because they'll no longer be distracted by financial problems." Is it to promote customer loyalty and brand? "...think about the types of employees you pay hourly, such as customer-service representatives and receptionists. These are the types of employees that have significant interaction with your customers and clients. They are the face of your company brand. It's important that they believe in your company, so they can do a great job in making your customers happy. After all, a happy customer is a repeat customer."[4] So long as your business is doing well, you want to make sure your employees are doing well. A happy employee is a good employee. Good employees lead to a successful business and compensation is the most important reward for a job well done.

Ultimately, there is no right or wrong answer as to when to give a raise. Employers should know their employees best in order to make that decision. Some other important factors to consider when

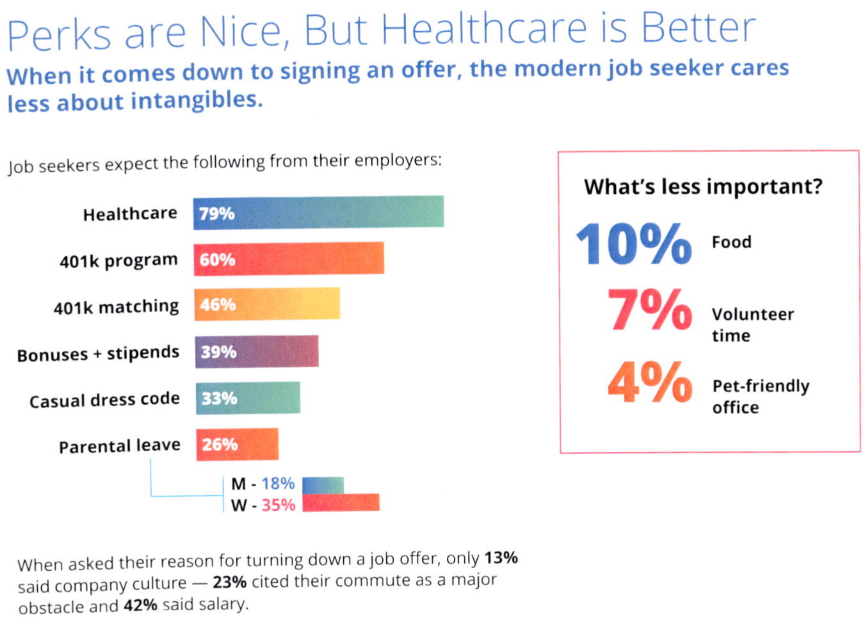

Information sourced from Jobvite.[3]

increasing salary and or benefits are consistent proficiency, continued outstanding contributions, constantly achieving or exceeding goals, and length of service. The goal of the employer, by giving pay and benefit increases, is to "reap the benefits of doing so, with advantages such as increased employee production, loyalty, and overall job satisfaction."[5]

Employees are your most valuable resource and you must incentivize employees to stay and do great jobs. "The high cost of employee turnover is something employers want to avoid. Not only is a high turnover rate financially damaging, there are intangible costs as well. If a company has a high employee turnover rate, work environment often suffers and staff morale may take a negative turn – insecurity can increase, motivation can slow, teamwork can be inhibited, and managers may lose the confidence of the work force."[5] Therefore, employers must put a lot of thought into their compensation, salary, and benefit structure, and the timeliness of salary and benefit increases that attract and retain the best employees for your organization. Employers should start with competitive compensation packages and try to increase compensation at least one time per year.

Salaries vs. Bonuses

When considering compensation for employees, one crucial factor to consider is whether or not you should give your employees a salary increase or offer them a bonus instead. For all practical purposes, a salary increase is forever—only in extreme situations, such as the immediate prospect of firm bankruptcy, would one decrease employee salaries. But a bonus is a one-shot gift—the bonus does not become a permanent part of the employees' base pay. And, the bonus can be large or small (or even zero) depending upon the fortunes of the firm.

So if your firm is doing well, you may want to consider an approach such as the following: give all employees a cost of living salary increase that tracks inflation (plus or minus a little, depending on your confidence that the inflation growth rate will continue or increase or decrease). Then, give out differential bonuses depending upon individual performance. Finally, look back at what you did last year. If firm performance was strong then, and if you think firm performance will continue, consider revising this year's bonus payouts by reducing some bonuses and turning those amounts into salary increases for the selected employees.

But of course, if your firm has a union, you will have to modify all the above depending upon what the union agreement stipulates. And in negotiating a union contract, seek maximum flexibility.

Major Takeaways

One thing that employers must avoid is increasing an employee salary just enough that puts the employee into the next higher tax bracket resulting in an employee taking home less money after taxes. In this instance, talk to your accountant and see if it is feasible to institute some sort of "cafeteria style" benefit plan that avoids less net take home pay due to higher tax brackets.

In addition, there is a continued push by many local and state governments to drastically increase the minimum wage. Of course, all minimum wage workers would hope this comes to fruition. But do minimum wage workers really hope for drastic increases in the minimum wage, or are they unwittingly pricing themselves out of a job? "Officials say San Francisco became the first major U.S. city to increase its minimum wage to $15 an hour under a ballot measure approved by voters in 2014. City Administrator Naomi Kelly says it will be the first to hit the milestone for all workers."[6]

The problem with unrealistic high wages for overvalued tasks is the ripple effect up the entire workforce ladder. If McDonald's cashiers and burger flippers, who just yesterday earned $7.35 per hour, are now *given* more than double that wage, then what does the $15 an hour employee deserve to be given? $30? These artificial arbitrary wages are not sustainable and will lead to inflation, unless the free private market innovation takes over to overcome government intrusion.

This is exactly what happened. In this instance, Wendy's introduced the first unmanned cashier kiosk and McDonald's implemented robotic burger flippers. In other words, if too many outside forces are exerted onto your business to artificially raise salaries and benefits, the employee risks being replaced, and the business must innovate to find other alternatives to perform the salaried tasks even better by different methods.

> "Wendy's (NASDAQ: WEN) has become the latest fast-food chain to partially replace its order-taking employees with a digital alternative. The company plans to add self-ordering kiosks at 1,000 locations by the end of the year, and executives noted during an analyst/investor day earlier this month that one benefit will be reducing labor costs.
>
> Chief Information Officer David Trimm also noted that kiosks would allow the company to serve more people during busier times. He said the kiosks pay for themselves in less than two years.

> "They are looking to improve their automation and their labor costs, and this is a good way to do it," Darren Tristano, vice president with Technomic, a food-service research and consulting firm, told The Associated Press. "They are also trying to enhance the customer experience. Younger customers prefer to use a kiosk." Trimm said during the analyst/investor day that "... everybody, whether you're a millennial or not, is now expecting to interact with brands via digital channels."
>
> Be it kiosks, mobile ordering via smartphone, or something else, it's very clear that in a number of fast-food and even fast-casual chains, technology can make it unnecessary to speak to a human being when placing an order. That will not only save money, it should also improve customer satisfaction."[7]

Therefore, as an employer, always reward the employee reasonably and competitively with the understanding and intention to consider lower cost technology to replace humans when the result will be less expensive and result in better customer service and quality outcomes.

Our consulting firm was tasked with the assistance of hiring staff for a technology company. We recruited independent contractors from around the country on a project by project basis in order to supplement the business employees that were already in place. We assessed the employee and contractor wage scales in the industry and saved the employer/business owner money by recommending that certain tasks can be done remotely from anywhere in the U.S. Based on this research, the employer started hiring independent contractors for certain projects saving the business up to 50% of wages per independent contractor hired. The employees and contractors were compensated appropriately based on their tasks and locations, concluding in successful projects and meeting goals.

References

1. Devon Thorsby. *The 25 Best Affordable Places to Live in the U.S. in 2018*. Apr. 2018. URL: realestate.usnews.com/real-estate/slideshows/best-affordable-places-to-live-in-the-us (cited on page 57).
2. Emmie Martin. *10 US Cities with High-Paying Jobs and a Low Cost of Living*. Mar. 2018. URL: www.cnbc.com/2018/02/27/us-cities-with-high-paying-jobs-and-low-cost-of-living.html (cited on page 58).
3. Jobvite. *2017 Job Seeker Nation Study: Finding the Fault Lines in the American Workforce*. 2017. URL: https://www.jobvite.com/wp-content/uploads/2017/05/2017_Job_Seeker_Nation_Survey.pdf (cited on pages 60, 61).
4. Andre Lavoie. *3 Reasons You Should Increase Employee Pay Now*. Oct. 2015. URL: www.entrepreneur.com/article/252039 (cited on page 60).
5. *How Often Should Employees Get Raises?* URL: https://www.villanovau.com/resources/hr/when-to-give-raises/ (cited on page 61).
6. Associated Press. *San Francisco Becomes 1st Major U.S. City with 15 Minimum Wage*. July 2018. URL: www.chicagotribune.com/business/ct-biz-san-francisco-minimum-wage-20180702-story.html (cited on page 62).

7. Daniel Kline. *Is the End Near for Fast-Food Workers?* Mar. 2017. URL: www.foxbusiness.com/markets/is-the-end-near-for-fast-food-workers (cited on page 63).

VIII Ready To Redesign, Repackage, Or Move Upmarket?

Overview

Is now the opportunity to redesign, repackage, or move upmarket for my business? Maybe, or maybe not.

According to the Merriam-Webster Dictionary, **redesign** is defined as:

- To revise in appearance, function, or content.

repackage is defined as:

- To package again or anew; specifically: to put into a more efficient or attractive form.

Finally, **upmarket** is defined as:

- Appealing or catering to high-income consumers; of high quality; not easily affordable or accessible.

Looking at the definitions of redesign, repackage, and upmarket, it would be most important to determine the *purpose* for any business decision. What are the *purposes* for any decisions to be made? First and foremost, why do businesses *package* and why do businesses *design*?

Repackaging and Redesigning

The most important reasons to package are to keep food fresh, to preserve, and to protect a product. Other important reasons would be to attract the consumer to your product and away from the competition. Packaging and design go hand in hand when deciding which marketplace pricing segment to enter:

- Premium
- Penetration
- Economy
- Skimming
- Psychological
- Neutral
- Captive
- Optional
- Bundling
- Promotional
- Geographical

Therefore, does your packaging meet the requirements for product freshness, protection, and safety, and does the design reflect your pricing and market demographics? These are the all-important questions to ask and answer when deciding on repackaging and/or redesigning.

For example, anyone who has purchased an Apple product within the last decade is aware of how beautiful the experience is of unboxing their products. Apple took the unusual step of hiring a team of designers that not only concentrated about how the package looks, but also created a sensory experience that reinforced its brand uniqueness even further. According to Adam Lashinsky, "Apple always wants to use the box that elicits the perfect emotional response on opening."[1]

> "*Sensory Experience.* It's not typically the first thing we think of when we think about marketing strategy. Yet sensory experience is the first experience customers have with your product: how the package looks. That sensory experience continues as they touch it and look at the images and text... Apple makes its packaging as artistic and visually appealing as the device inside. Every corner of the box is clean, the color is an elegant, minimalist white. How does Apple create that experience? By giving as much attention to the 'small stuff' as they do the big stuff. The inexpensive box gets as much attention as the expensive devices inside. To ensure that opening the box is a unique experience, Apple employs a designer whose sole job is packaging. The company also has a designer who is devoted to opening hundreds of prototype boxes. That designer creates and tests endless versions of box shape, angles and tapes. This isn't just about aesthetics. It's also about a package that's easy for customers to open, easy for them to identify the component parts, and easy for them to start using. It's a process that's focused on the customer – not on, say, preventing shoplifting.
>
> In His book, "Inside Apple," Adam Lashinsky's says: "To fully grasp how seriously Apple executives sweat the small stuff, consider this: For months, a packaging designer was holed up in this room performing the most mundane of tasks – opening boxes." "One after another, the designer created and tested an endless series of arrows, colors, and tapes for a tiny tab designed to show the consumer where to pull back the invisible, full-bleed sticker adhered to the top of the clear iPod box. Getting it just right was this particular designer's obsession... I come away from this thinking two things. First, I'm glad that this happens. Rightly or wrongly, I still get excited whenever I open an Apple product. In fact, I get a little excited when anyone opens something from Apple. Second: I'm glad I'm not an Apple packaging designer."[2]

The result of this focus is that one-of-a-kind experience of unpacking an Apple product. It demonstrates intense attention to detail. "The label may help customers decide whether to buy, but if the packaging doesn't engage them, chances are they're not going to buy."[2] This set themselves apart from everyone else in order to make its brand unique and elevate its brands' perceived value. They wanted you to experience their product and how great it is even before they used it; vacuum packed, fresh, not tempered with, brand new. According to Scott Young, "Visibility is directly connected to purchase levels... It's a key reason 80 percent of new retail products fail. Visual contrast to other brands is the key..."[2]

Here are four tips that apply the package design principles that will help build your brand which has been so effective for Apple's brand reported by *Personalics*:

1. Design from the outside in. Put package design at the top of the priority list, not at the bottom. Spend as much time unpacking your boxes as you do figuring out how to pack them.
2. Break the rules. Create a conventional package design and make a list of its characteristics. Then make a list of the opposites of those characteristics and experiment with using them in your package design. Use color in uncharacteristic ways – resist visual clichés such as using black to convey "high tech" or unbleached cardboard to communicate "natural," says Ted Mininni of packaging and licensing design firm Design Force.
3. After you decide what could go on the box, start taking things take off. Focus on differentiators that set your brand apart.
4. Imitate the best. Creative Bloq has an extensive list of packaging design resources to get

your creative juices running.[2]

Let's look at repackaging first. Is the product in the best package available for the longest shelf life, least destructiveness, and safety tampering? If you have the opportunity to increase shelf life by repackaging or place the product in a package that will hold up better to weather and crushing forces or to better promote safety, then do it, so long it is cost effective. Too often, products come in flimsy packaging and don't do the product justice. The package specifications and style do play a vital role in consumer decisions. Consumers do not want to purchase a product, later to find the packaging crushed or open at the bottom of the shopping bag when they return home or office. Also, if you participate in ecommerce or ship your product, make sure it holds up well to shipping and is light weight. Why pay for breakable heavy glass or overpriced shipping when non-breakable, lightweight, recyclable plastic can be used? Always think of the integrity of the packaging providing the consumer a great first impression and being reflective of the product quality inside the package. Packaging style and integrity do help sell products!

Once you are committed to the *repackage* style and integrity, you now have the new palette to work with for the redesign. Think of your new package as a blank canvas to recreate and promote your product, business, and brand with words, logos, information, photos, images and vibrant colors. You want your design to identifiably "pop" and "jump out" at the consumer. You want your packaged product to "stand out" from the rest, while sitting on the shelf to be purchased. Think about what you need to do to make your product and package the first choice for consumers. Clear communication of the product, its uniqueness, mission, and its special characteristics are essential to any successful redesign.

A redesign might also be necessary in order to stay relevant in a very competitive growing market. Be able to communicate exactly what consumers are looking for and would want from your product. If you are looking to grow beyond your current distribution area, then brand awareness must be an essential addition to your redesign. Quality and benefits of the product should be clearly represented displayed in the brand name or slogan for more easy shop-ability and improved brand awareness. When doing a redesign, be sure to capitalize on any product or brand reputation, history, community and successes while portraying top credibility. If there is a way to incorporate consumer lifestyle in the redesign process, take advantage of that sort of messaging. Consumers will sooner buy a product or brand that they can identify with or feel they will incorporate in their everyday lifestyle or special occasions.

A redesign can also include the elimination of packaging, such as the outer box. This could save money, portray that your company is sustainable, ecofriendly, and allow the product to be more visible on the shelf; while taking up less shelf space resulting in more room for more of your product placement.

The following is the perfect quote demonstrating necessary strategic design changes of their packaging, from a satisfied CEO, on their redesign project.

> According to Stuart Whitworth, partner/chief creative officer, Flood Creative, 'The positioning change and lifestyle connection required a complete overhaul to reflect consumers' everyday use of the product. We started by making the brand identity more approachable by replacing the formal and almost calligraphic script with a modern, casual black script. It's still confident but now more personal. The new script combined with the lower-case initials and the slight angle at which the brand name is written all come together to reflect more of how we write today. The gold shell is a new icon we created and is now a permanent part of the bolder and more expressive logo.'[3]

If 3-D visualization, imagination, creativity, and/or design thinking are not your strong suits, turn to experts. Consultants frequently refer to and/or employ design agencies such as Frog, IDEO, and Woods Bagot. Talk with your consultant to see whom they recommend.

Going Upmarket

Now consider going *upmarket*. Is your product and packaging of high quality, does it possess at least one unique property or characteristic, and does it have a higher perceived value than your competitors? If so, it's time to go upmarket. Consider a strategy for increasing the purchase price to the consumer's perceived value within the higher range of what the market would bear. The following are examples of some international upmarket brands:[4]

- Burberry
- Cartier
- Chanel
- Fendi
- Gucci
- Hennessy
- Hermès
- Moët & Chandon
- Rolex
- Louis Vuitton
- Mercedes
- BMW
- Audi
- Range Rover
- Rolls-Royce
- Porsche
- Bentley
- Jaguar

Each upmarket luxury brand has a certain "panache" quality and marketing strategy that must be different than mainstream. With this being said, what is that special upmarket brand marketing strategy? A marketing expert calls it "the anti-laws of marketing." "In fact, we coined the term anti-law of marketing to designate the counter-intuitive managerial principles, which made these brands command their incredible pricing power and margins...if you decide to implement a fashion or a premium strategy, the classical marketing styles works pretty well. But if you decide to implement a luxury strategy, you need to reconsider all the aspects of your marketing management."[5]

Premium and *fashion* strategies are simple and routine. They are defined by comparison of quality, price, and desirable fashion. To the contrary, luxury pricing is more complex and leverages the intangibles of: time, heritage, origin, craftsmanship, hand-made, small batches, celebrity, and prestigious clientele.

When choosing to enter the luxury upmarket pricing, it is imperative that you know your customers and their demographics. Before you do any repackaging, redesign, or upmarket planning, you must know the groups and individuals who you are up marketing to. By knowing their:

- Characteristics and needs
- Wants
- Tastes

- Preferred colors
- Packaging material preferences
- Age range
- Gender
- Race
- Ethnicity

you can be ahead of the game by tailoring the repackaged and redesigned look to that luxury priced market that you are targeting, in addition to the other demographics who cannot afford to purchase the product, but who will help you market it by talking about it with others and hopefully creating a media buzz. Sometimes, those who do not purchase the product and are envious telling everyone they will buy the product when they can afford it are your best marketers.[6]

Takeaway Lessons

Apple is not considered a "luxury brand" and it appeals to everyone, but it does apply the principles to capture upmarket luxury pricing. Apple has figured out the way to achieve the best of both worlds in the mobile phone and computer markets, the non-luxury commodity that sells to the masses, and at luxury pricing. In fact, Apple is the first company in world history to achieve a one trillion-dollar market capitalization. Observe how they do it. They have: a quality brand with quality packaging, excellent R&D, and perceived value, selling through select retailers at the same "manufacturers' suggested retail price," and devices with brand awareness that are needed and integrate into a customer's everyday life. When possible, the luxury strategy is often the best business model to implement for many products and services by setting yourself apart from your competition and trying to achieve the highest profitability.

Let's take an extreme example of up marketing an everyday $2 container of applesauce. For one of our clients we chose an elegant expensive looking tall olive style jar with a gold gap for packaging, dressed the jar up with an upscale wine style label for design, made the applesauce all natural, changed the name on the label from something downmarket such as "Fred's Applesauce" to something more upmarket such as "Organic Apple Splendor," sourced the apples locally, left the apple peel in for nutrients and texture, and you now have a $9 jar of applesauce. See how planning for upmarket can earn you a 450% increase in retail pricing on a single product?

As you can see, if any of these product repackaging, redesign or upmarket approaches are lacking in your present product, it would be a good time to consider repackaging, redesign, and/or upmarket strategies. Similar repackage, redesign, and upmarket concepts can also be applied to the entire business as is done with a product or brand. "... the fundamental rethinking and radical redesign of business processes to achieve dramatic improvements in critical contemporary modern measures of performance, such as cost, quality, service, and speed."[7]

So, when you think about repackaging or redesigning your business for the upmarket, think about your business as a product and apply those same principles. In order to accomplish a more upmarket "luxury looking" business, it will need a re-brand. A successful rebrand will reintroduce the "new" business, acquire former clients, target the ideal demographic, and generate higher sales and bigger profits.

The key to rebranding for upmarket is to reposition your business in order to grow and penetrate new markets. Regain the trust and respect that might have been lacking in the past and reposition your business and brand for future prosperity. Build on the already existing products and services offered and decide whether it is best to rebrand expeditiously if your current brand is a detriment to sales, or to do a slow methodical rollout to build on an already positive known brand. As you are repackaging the business, share all positive information as your marketing tools. Contact the media with press releases; sharing your story, new products or services, introducing new staff, photographs, and offer on premises interviews. You will be surprised how receptive the press can be and consider your story as newsworthy.

When consulting for a Cuban restaurant, our firm was responsible for a re-opening and rebrand. We scheduled the local congressman to do the ribbon cutting and themed the story on an immigrant from Cuba, who fled Cuba due to political artwork persecution, and is now renovating and staffing his restaurant and supporting the local economy. The place was packed for the opening, with tremendous press coverage. The rebrand was a success.

Maintain and rebrand the business periodically due to: innovation, new products and services, new location, new owners or managers, and changing times and environment. Always project to your customers that the business and its staff stay up to date. Upmarket rebranding works well in the cosmetic services professions. Clientele are always interested and will be fully engaged when appearance is involved. Customers are always interested in the newest technology and doctors available for cosmetic surgery. Repackaging, redesign, and upmarket strategies can never be overemphasized and underestimated. Always look for every excuse to communicate with your customers to generate more business and new referrals through rebranding and upmarket methods and tactics.

References

1. Jamie Condliffe. *Apple's Packaging Is So Good Because It Employs a Dedicated Box Opener*. June 2013. URL: gizmodo.com/5879097/apple-packing-is-so-good-because-they-employ-a-dedicated-box-opener (cited on page 68).
2. *How packaging gives Apple's buyers a sensory experience that reinforces brand*. Mar. 2016. URL: https://www.personalics.com/2016/02/03/sensory-design-packaging/ (cited on pages 68, 69).
3. Kristin Joker. *Napkin Redesign Serves Everyday Purpose*. Mar. 2018. URL: https://www.brandpackaging.com/articles/86164-napkin-redesign-serves-everyday-purpose (cited on page 69).
4. *Best Luxury Cars*. URL: www.carbuyer.co.uk/reviews/recommended/best-luxury-cars (cited on page 70).
5. Vincent Bastien. *Marketing To A High-End Consumer, Using The Luxury Strategy*. Sept. 2015. URL: www.entrepreneur.com/article/250745 (cited on page 70).
6. *Items Tagged with 'packaging redesign'*. URL: www.brandpackaging.com/keywords/2359-packaging-redesign (cited on page 71).
7. Will Kenton. *Business Process Redesign (BPR)*. Dec. 2017. URL: https://www.investopedia.com/terms/b/business-process-redesign.asp (cited on page 71).

IX

Time To Expand My Business And Market Presence

Overview

Is now the opportunity to expand my business and market presence? According to the dictionary by Merriam-Webster, *expand* is defined as:

- To increase in extent, size, volume, scope.
- To spread or stretch out; unfold.
- To express in fuller form or greater detail.

Expanding a business is exciting and fun, especially when the pitfalls are avoided, and profits are plentiful. This chapter will provide successful guidance and help you avoid common mistakes.

Readiness

Remember the old adage, "bigger is NOT always better." Too rapid growth can kill a business. It can spiral out of control because of "...complexity. Operations become increasingly complex as companies launch new products, enter new markets, and pursue new customers. In a survey of 300 executives by the Economist Intelligence Unit, nearly 90 percent of respondents said complexity was raising their overall costs.[1] This common complaint reflects the inescapable reality that growth breeds complexity. It's not a choice — with few exceptions, most growing companies become more complex. Every new product, market, or channel brings costly new requirements in areas such as product design, customer service expectations, and even production and distribution assets. Managing these variables without losing control of costs is a central challenge for every growing business."[2] It is best to generate a business, mastering its strong core foundation. Make sure all the "opportunity" fundamentals in this guide are fully developed and implemented before business expansion. It is easy to arbitrarily add to a business, but nearly impossible to take back noticeable and harmful mistakes.

So, are you really ready to grow your business and expand market presence? The Wharton School of Business has an executive education program which addresses these requisite questions of "scaling ventures." Wharton suggests that one "determine whether or not your company's existing operational structure and capabilities are ready to scale:"[2]

- Stress test current organizational structure and processes to discover readiness to grow
- Identify and measure the key performance indicators needed for scaling
- Create a financially viable, scalable strategic plan
- Discover how to drive innovation to stimulate growth
- Understand the capital requirements needed to grow and how to attain them
- Balance people and processes to achieve successful strategy execution

According to Deloitte's three-part series on creating sustainable and scalable improvements to a business's cost structure, the first step is rethinking the company's business model. This provides the blueprint for the effort. Determining how decisions will be made serve as a strong foundation, "aligning and improving the way decisions are made and executed." Finally, "Redefine functional service delivery to achieve organizational scalability and efficiency." This explains different ways companies can expand their resources, so they can create a cost structure and continue improvements in performance which capture the businesses specific needs.[3]

Planning for Growth

As a result, a business should develop an actionable plan to scale your organization. If your company is ready to expand in the marketplace, then The Wharton School of Business recommends that you develop a plan that will address:[4]

- Avoiding explosions: building and leading successful teams
- Balancing people and processes
- Metrics for scaling
- Managing assets for growth
- Local to global: managing global networks (simulation)
- Scaling through innovation
- Financing the growing business
- Scaling up quality: hiring, leading, and organizing for success
- Value creation in fast growth companies

According to an article that was originally published by Booz & Company, there are three common trends companies had for a sustainable course of high performance and continued growth. They:

- Create clarity and coherence within their strategy and articulate the capabilities that they need in order to win in the marketplace
- Put in place an optimized cost structure and approach to capital allocation
  - Include continual investment in the capabilities that are critical to success
  - Proactively cut costs in less-critical areas to fund these investments
- Build supportive organizations

What Booz & Company means is that these companies redesign their structures, skill sets, and other organizational and cultural elements to align more with their behavior to their strategy, and to tackle the collective actions of their people.[5]

Expanding presence will encounter many obstacles, is difficult, and will affect every facet of the business. However, when done properly with hard work and educated risk-taking, expansion can yield huge rewards. With strong leadership, navigating direction is most important. When a project loses direction, it derails and fails. Good leadership will stay on top of every detail. No detail is too small to consider and supervise. An unattended small detail can spiral out of control and adversely affect your growth plans. Once the business growth leadership team is in place, set out the financial plan. Where will the "growth" money come from? Growth does not come without expense. As the saying goes, businesses must "spend money to make money." Lastly, set out the entire strategic plan in writing. This should be an addendum to the original business plan. In addition, now is the time to update the business plan and evaluate what worked and what did not. These three elements are critical to successful growth. If one element is compromised, growing your venture becomes much more difficult or nearly impossible.

The growth strategic plan will help to "determine which approach to growth is most viable for your organization, transition for that growth, and be able to communicate an action plan that addresses strategic, financial, and leadership concerns."[4] The strategic plan should set out to identify "what type of organizational culture a company needs to have to grow and how to define the role of the company's founder or owner/operator as the firm embarks on this new phase of growth."[3] Finally, the leadership team must "consider whether the current strategy is scalable from both the execution and financial viewpoints, and also examine the risks inherent to your plan and analyze how to build the right portfolio of processes, assets, and people to address those risks."[3]

There are different ways to grow a business: add new products or services, sell more of the same products or services, add new territories or regions, target additional demographics, expand distribution channels, and merger or acquisition.[6]

Six Different Modalities of Growth

1. Add new products and services to your mix.

This strategy sounds relatively simple, but executing it well can be challenging. For starters, you need to figure out which products and services your customers want, and how much they'll be willing to pay for them. Next, determine whether or not you can sell these products and services at a profit.

The best way to accomplish this is to conduct thorough market research before committing any resources (financial or human) to new product or service expansion. Ask your current customers what they think about your new product and service ideas, including potential price points. Your market research needs to focus on customer demand for new products and services and your cost to manufacture, deliver, and sell them.

2. Sell more products and services to your existing customers.

This is the flip side of the first strategy: Penetrating deeper into your current customer base. Start by performing a market segmentation analysis to identify the customer segments that are more likely to buy so you can focus your sales and marketing efforts on these segments.

This analysis will divide your customers into segments based on the criteria you choose (age, gender, location, buying history, etc.) so you can analyze their potential profitability when it comes to selling them new products and services. Armed with this information, you can better allocate your sales and marketing dollars.

3. Expand into new territories.

The idea here is to market and sell your existing products and services to new customers. These new customers can be in different segments or niches or different locations from where you currently operate.

If yours is a retail or storefront business, this type of expansion will likely involve opening new locations in different geographic areas— whether across town or across the country. Doing so will require a significant investment of both time and money, so perform thorough market research first to make sure there is enough customer demand in the new territory to justify the expansion.

"When you are thinking about expanding into new areas, the first thing you need to do is to determine how to specialize your advertising for your new market," advises Tri Nguyen, founder and CEO of Network Capital Funding Corporation. "If you can't convey the benefits of your product or service to residents of a new region, you're going to struggle to make it. Be honest about flaws and strengths as you consider the message you will be conveying to a new area."[6]

4. Target new customer markets.

Most businesses target their sales and marketing efforts to specific customer markets based on demographics like age, gender, and location or psychographics like interests, activities, and values. But are there other customer markets that might also be viable for your products and services?

"Being able to reach the right target customers through the right mediums, at the right time, is the first step to expanding your business into new customer markets," says Network Capital's Nguyen. "When expanding into new target markets, you need to ramp up your advertising to these markets. This is pretty intuitive, but it's true."[6]

5. Tap into new sales and delivery channels.

The Internet is the best example of how a new sales and delivery channel can transform a small business. Countless companies have reinvented themselves to take advantage of online opportunities — from brick-and-mortar retailers opening online stores to service providers who are able to reach a much broader audience by advertising online and using search engine optimization (SEO) techniques to rank highly in Web searches conducted by the prospective customers.

6. Acquire another business.

This may be the fastest route to growth and expansion, but it may also be the fastest route to ruin. Merging with or acquiring another business can double the size of your business overnight, growing your sales and revenue exponentially. But you must perform thorough due diligence on any potential acquisition candidates before moving forward with a business merger.

In particular, your due diligence efforts should focus on the company's financial condition, the strength and depth of its management team, the breadth of its client base, and the soundness of existing contracts. When considering companies to possibly acquire, look for synergies between the two businesses that will result in the combined entity being stronger than either of the individual businesses would be standing on their own.

The condition of the economy does not have to dictate your business growth and expansion plans. Consider how you can implement one or more of these strategies to put your company on the fast track to expansion today.

But beware – some 70% of mergers and acquisitions fail in some crucial manner. See our chapter on mergers and acquisitions for more details.

To illustrate more details involved in expansion, take a look at two in a bit more detail: product line expansion and territorial expansion. Similar considerations surface in undertaking any of the other four expansion modalities.[6]

Product Line Expansion

When considering a new product expansion; save money and do market research first. Test the product or service on some of your already existing customers, ask them if they would purchase it, and at what price points. When wanting to increase sales volumes, figure out who is buying each type of product or service. By decompartmentalizing sales of certain items into specific groups, you can target your marketing to specific groups for the certain items that sell best to those groups. For example, you would be target marketing perfume to women, cologne to men, or the general fragrance product to all individuals around seasonal holiday times as gift ideas or at birthday times if you collected that data. Armed with this information of customers, these data would divide your customers into groups based on:

- Age
- Hobbies
- Gender
- Schooling level
- Race
- Location
- Ethnicity
- Income
- Marital status
- Buying history

Now, you can better forecast sales and profitability of the new products and services that are being considered for commerce.

Territorial Expansion

Expanding into new territories could involve: renting or purchasing property, driving your mobile business into new areas, and listing your products and services on additional internet platforms or websites. Expanding into new target markets requires "Being able to reach the right target customers through the right mediums, at the right time, is the first step to expanding your business into new customer markets," says Network Capital's Nguyen. "When expanding into new target markets, you need to ramp up your advertising to these markets. This is pretty intuitive, but it's true." New distribution channels are prevalent today. With the internet, channels are diverse and virtually unlimited due to a wide array of different: websites, social media, and e-commerce sites. Merging with, or acquiring another company is another way to grow your business, and the fastest. This choice of growth mandates that "due diligence efforts should focus on the company's financial condition, the strength and depth of its management team, the breadth of its client base, and the soundness of existing contracts. When considering companies to possibly acquire, look for synergies between the two businesses that will result in the combined entity being stronger than either of the individual businesses would be standing on its own."[6]

Always "Consider how you can implement one or more of these strategies to put your company on the fast track to expansion," but only, when it's the right time to grow the business.[6]

Major Takeaway

When you are presented an opportunity to grow your business, take it seriously, exercise due diligence, and hire consultants to assess the growth potential and the risk. Having said this, how could a company named at the time, "Excite," now known as "ask.com, decline to acquire and merge with "Google for a measly $750,000; about the price of a house? No doubt, this is the WORST business decision in history. Google is now worth $365 billion today. This would have been a 487,000% return on investment. Don't be foolish and let these opportunities pass you by.[7]

References

1. *The Complexity Challenge: How businesses are bearing up*. The Economist Intelligence Unit, 2011. URL: http://www.eiu.com/report_dl.asp?mode=fi&fi=1367778921.pdf (cited on page 75).
2. K.B. Clausen and Richard Kauffeld. *Winning with complexity: Operations capabilities that drive profitable growth*. Aug. 2014. URL: https://www.strategyand.pwc.com/report/winning-with-complexity (cited on page 75).
3. Omar Aguilar and Rick Ferraro. *Three steps to sustainable and scalable change. Part 3: Redefining functional service delivery to achieve organizational scalability and efficiency*. SCT Eminence Series. Deloitte Development, 2016. URL: https://www2.deloitte.com/content/dam/Deloitte/us/Documents/process-and-operations/us-deloitte-operations-eminence-part-three.pdf (cited on pages 76, 77).
4. Allon Gad. *Scaling Ventures: Developing the Playbook for Profitable Growth*. URL: https://executiveeducation.wharton.upenn.edu/for-individuals/all-programs/scaling-ventures-developing-the-playbook-for-profitable-growth/ (cited on pages 76, 77).
5. Ashok Divakaran and Vinay Couto. *How Ready Are You for Growth?* Online. Booz & Co., June 2013 (cited on page 76).
6. Don Sadler. *6 Tips for Expanding Your Business – Regardless of the Economy*. July 2014. URL: https://www.allbusiness.com/expanding-your-business-regardless-of-economy-16435-1.html (cited on pages 77, 78, 80).
7. Jason Nazar. *The Biggest Business Blunders in History*. Nov. 2013 (cited on page 80).

X

Should I Insource Or Outsource My Products?

Overview

According to the Merriam-Webster Dictionary, *insource* is defined as to:

1. "procure (something, such as goods or services needed by a business or organization) from domestic or in-house sources rather than from foreign or outside suppliers: to contract for work, jobs, etc., to be done by in-house or domestic workers"

Outsource is defined as:

1. (a company or organization) to purchase (goods) or subcontract (services) from an outside supplier or source.
2. to contract out (jobs, services, etc.):

What is meant by "insourcing" and "outsourcing?" Insourcing is the "Assigning a project to a person or department within the company instead of hiring an outside person or company to do the work. While outsourcing is commonly thought of as a way for companies to save money, it is sometimes more cost effective to have the work done in-house [...] In the United States, insourcing can also refer to the use of U.S.-based subsidiaries by foreign multinational corporations. These insourcing companies contribute to research and development, capital investment, exports and job creation. So, while outsourcing is often looked upon as a negative effect of globalization that sends U.S. jobs abroad to countries with cheaper labor, outsourcing actually works both ways because it also sends jobs to the United States from foreign countries."[1]

Outsourcing is "the practice of having certain job functions done outside a company instead of having an in-house department or employee handle them; functions can be outsourced to either a company or an individual. Outsourcing has become a major trend in human resources..."[2]

INSOURCING IS BEST FOR	OUTSOURCING IS BEST FOR
Non-commodity products (specialized, small-volume components or devices).	Commodity products (uniform, large-volume components or devices).
New products that could require numerous updates or improvements.	Established products that do not require many design iterations.
Products for an unstable or finite market.	Products that have established markets.
Mid- or large-sized OEMs with manufacturing facilities.	Small OEMs with limited capital.
Reducing supply-chain costs and focusing on control of quality.	Reducing labor costs and concentrating on core competencies.

Using Insourcing and Outsourcing

How do "insourcing" and "outsourcing" fit into your business strategy? Well, that depends on the type of business and project. The way a business is structured, and the type of projects undertaken, will determine which is more profitable and yield a better-quality outcome. One outsourcing extreme would be the sole proprietor. How much can one person do? When more business comes in than can be handled, the business might think it has two choices:

1. The business can put the project in a queue and complete the project as soon as possible with projects first in line still ahead to complete, or
2. Outsource the project for expeditious completion.

In reality, in the real business world, unless it's government, the client wants projects completed yesterday. To your client, "time is money." The longer it takes you to complete the project, the further business opportunity lost. This could then lead to less revenue produced which would result in lost profits. The same holds true for your business. The faster your turnover of projects; the more profit your business makes, the more your customers are satisfied, and the less likely your customers are to leave your business looking for quicker results.

Many small and large companies outsource for higher profits. When you do not have the inside staff to complete a client project, it can be cheaper to outsource the project than hire new employees and have to pay more: salaries, payroll taxes, benefits, training costs, office space costs, etc. By outsourcing, your business has more flexibility to take on various and significantly different projects which require different skill sets. It is not practical to hire a new employee every time a specialized project comes in. Your business can actually provide faster, higher quality, and more cost-effective products and services by outsourcing and following certain common-sense guidelines that include:

- Reference checking of the subcontractor or outsource company.
- Deadline agreements.
- Subcontractor work orders and contracts specifying the work for hire.
- Confidentiality agreements to protect your and your client's intellectual property.
- Insurance coverage with your company and client as an additional insured on the subcontractor policy.
- Able to meet expectations and quality requirements.
- Good communication skills.

On the flip side of outsourcing, the number one reason to insource is for greater flexibility. "...cost-effectiveness is not just a low-cost labor calculation, but an effective – and cost-effective – integration of a service or tool into the company's existing environment...The answer will lie in the network of related services and the ability to better control ongoing change. The most common insourcing decisions we see these days are driven by that desire for greater flexibility."[3] Insourcing to increase brand value is also a factor since "most people would prefer to buy from a company that creates local jobs, all else being equal. There can be marketing and goodwill value far beyond the modest increase in cost that insourcing might represent."[3] When you know that you can complete a project just as well or better, by in-housing, then keep the project in-house and insource. When you "can demonstrate your results truly were better in-house"[3] let these projects continue to be performed in-house.

When beating the competition is crucial and there are unique capabilities involved, do NOT outsource. "You may have a better chance of protecting your intellectual property by keeping key, differentiating capabilities in house ...We are seeing situations where clients insource certain functions related to industry-specific business expertise and intellectual capital. These can include thought leadership functions such as architecture and business analysis. Some clients find that outsourcing those areas creates a challenge for knowledge retention and competitive differentiation."[3] Creating leadership and building a first-class team within the company is a huge advantage moving forward. "Keeping some things in house in order to build tomorrow's leaders could be a good idea, as long as you know how to recognize, retain, and reward them."[3]

Bottom line, here are the two basic questions:

1. Can I do it better/faster/cheaper than the market?
2. Should I worry about doing it better/faster/cheaper than the market?[3]

"Most things that get outsourced need to be stable, reliable, and compliant, but not top notch. Paying for best in class is often a waste of money because the market may not reward you for it."[3]

Major Takeaway

A few great outsourcing decisions includes Samsung and their decision to launch a sabbatical program which sends their top talent around the world. This is what continues to be the secret behind Samsung's success as a global brand.[4]

> "Product companies, such as P&G, have a big challenge performing in a very rapidly changing market. It is critical to bring out a new product ahead of many competitors. So one day, after decades of product race, P&G made a decision to outsource some R&D activities. The result exceeded all the expectations. Outsourcing boosted its innovation productivity by 60% and generated more than $10 billion in revenue from over 400 new products. Today, about half of P&G's innovation comes from external collaboration."[5]
>
> Unilever, "not being a specialist in IT solutions, the company outsourced the development of ERP system to external party. As a result, these improvements have directly contributed to the € 700 million annual savings on operational activities."[5]

In addition, businessman and entrepreneur Mark McRae professes "Outsourcing can give you access to a dizzying array of highly skilled professionals from all over the world. For example, to produce a professional documentary, I hired a script writer in the USA, film crew from Canada, post-production team in Croatia and editor in Serbia."[5]

> "The Acer executives knew it was good at branding and marketing and chose to outsource everything company had a harder time with, like manufacturing. The move led Acer to faster-growing sales and gains in market share. The company now maintains a strikingly lean and flexible operation. Its 6,800 employees represent a workforce less than a tenth the size of its largest competitor."[5]
>
> "JM Family Enterprises is a diversified automotive corporation whose principal businesses focus on vehicle distribution and processing, financial services, and technology products. The company outsourced all mainframe hardware, software, and operations once mainframe usage leveled off at $8.2 billion. The outsourcing

> vendor immediately optimized operations so that critical month-end financial reports landed on the desks of JM Family executives on time, which hadn't happened before."[5]

These success stories prove that proper strategy and decision making can result in greater than expected results. The greatest insource decisions were those of General Electric and Ford. "Jack Welch's (General Electric) decision to fully fund a first-in-class training center at Crotonville, led to the development of hundreds of great leaders who practiced the "GE Way."[4]

"Henry Ford's (Ford Motor Company) decision to double the wages of his workers enabled him to attract the talent he needed, and helped insure a class of worker who could afford the very products they were building."[4]

These insourcing decisions were vital to retaining great talent and creating great leaders. More favorable changes in the global economy are bringing insourcing back. These are examples favoring insourcing vs outsourcing:

1. Oil prices are three times what they were in 2000, making cargo-ship fuel much more expensive now than it was then.
2. The natural-gas boom in the U.S. has dramatically lowered the cost for running something as energy-intensive as a factory here at home. (Natural gas now costs four times as much in Asia as it does in the U.S.)
3. In dollars, wages in China are some five times what they were in 2000—and they are expected to keep rising 18 percent a year.
4. American unions are changing their priorities. Appliance Park's union was so fractious in the '70s and '80s that the place was known as "Strike City." That same union agreed to a two-tier wage scale in 2005—and today, 70 percent of the jobs there are on the lower tier, which starts at just over $13.50 an hour, almost $8 less than what the starting wage used to be.
5. United States labor productivity has continued its long march upward, meaning that labor costs have become a smaller and smaller proportion of the total cost of finished goods. You simply can't save much money chasing wages anymore."[6]

Our firm was hired by an award-winning photographer and art gallery curator whose work is in the world-famous Smithsonian Institute in Washington, DC. We were asked for assistance on the client's photography book content. We looked at the current marketplace and demographics, then recommended a particular industry. The client normally makes all of their calls and arrangements. However, in this instance, our client was not familiar with the industry and felt uncomfortable making the calls. Therefore, having clients in the industry already, our client outsourced all the photoshoots and logistics to our firm. Within one week, everything was scheduled for the very particular weeks of the year that this type of photography can take place.

Later that year, we arrived for a seven-day photoshoot with interviews. The networking and visit arranged by the outsourced consultant was a success. Two years later, the client's photography book was published and critically acclaimed. This is the perfect example when a business owner or professional must realize they can't always "wear all the hats". Certain obligations are better outsourced in someone else's hands for better efficiency, productivity, and success.

References

1. Will Kenton. *Insourcing*. June 2018. URL: https://www.investopedia.com/terms/i/insourcing.asp (cited on page 83).
2. Matt Weinberger, Stephen J. Bronner, and Anna Johansson. *Outsourcing Definition - Entrepreneur Small Business Encyclopedia*. URL: http://www.entrepreneur.com/encyclopedia/outsourcing (cited on page 83).
3. Bianca Wright. *Five Scenarios Where Insourcing Makes Better Sense Than Outsourcing*. June 2015. URL: http://www.nearshoreamericas.com/scenarios-insourcing-sense-outsourcing/ (cited on pages 84, 85).
4. Kevin Kruse. *The Top 5 Business Decisions Of All Time*. May 2013. URL: https://www.forbes.com/sites/kevinkruse/2013/05/22/business-decisions/ (cited on pages 85, 86).
5. Anna Muzychko. *5 Successful Stories of Outsourcing*. June 2015. URL: https://www.linkedin.com/pulse/5-successful-stories-outsourcing-anna-muzychko/ (cited on pages 85, 86).
6. Charles Fishman. *The Insourcing Boom*. Dec. 2012. URL: http://www.theatlantic.com/magazine/archive/2012/12/the-insourcing-boom/309166/. (cited on page 86).

XI Establishing Long Term Contracts

Overview

Is now the opportunity to establish long-term contracts? Good question. Is it time to lock in terms for an extended amount of time, or not?

What is a *contract*?

According to the Merriam-Webster Dictionary, a *contract* is defined as:

1. An agreement between two or more parties for the doing or not doing of something specified.
2. An agreement enforceable by law.
3. The written form of such an agreement.

Contracting with other parties for long periods of time is a double-edged sword. On the one hand, both parties might want to lock in terms that are favorable at the time. On the other hand, things change and might not be so favorable down the road. Consider what conditions make for favorable long-term agreements: many companies can make the case that a service contract was better for customers than hiring on a "one-off" basis. This is a win-win for everyone. When a client has a need, the company is "on retainer" to fix the "problem." Make one phone call and the problem is solved. There is no searching for anyone who might be available to handle the issue. (But there is no guarantee the problem will be solved, or even if the company representative will show up for the appointment.) But in general, clients are happy because they have a problem solver on call, and the company that is providing the product or service is happy because it is pre-sold with money in hand for future service. Contracted services in general provide faster, shorter turnaround, lower priced, preventative, quality services.[1]

Simple long-term contracts are found between businesses and end user customers (e.g., residential plumbing services). More complicated long-term contracts are found between two businesses (e.g., stipulations on number of products or service calls, on quality, on response time to resolve problems, etc.). To a certain extent, warranties and guarantees can be considered to be a type of long-term contract.

The provider of the long-term service or product contract usually prefers this type of arrangement for any of several reasons:[2]

- Mastering of strategies and routines
- Better return on investment
- Reduced operating costs
- Dedicated account support
- Upgrade of service quality
- Stronger partnerships
- Same staff and increased security

When contracting, you are either on the providing or receiving end of goods or services in exchange for monetary payment, or some sort of consideration. There are technically, several different types of contracts (written, verbal, promissory estoppel, express, implied, etc.). A contract is "An agreement, upon sufficient consideration, to do or not to do a particular thing... A covenant or agreement between two or more persons, with a lawful consideration or cause. A deliberate engagement between competent parties, upon a legal consideration, to do or abstain from doing, some act. A contract or agreement is either where a promise is made on one side and assented to on the other, or where two or more persons enter into engagement with each other by a promise on either side... A contract is an agreement by which one party obligates himself to another to give, to

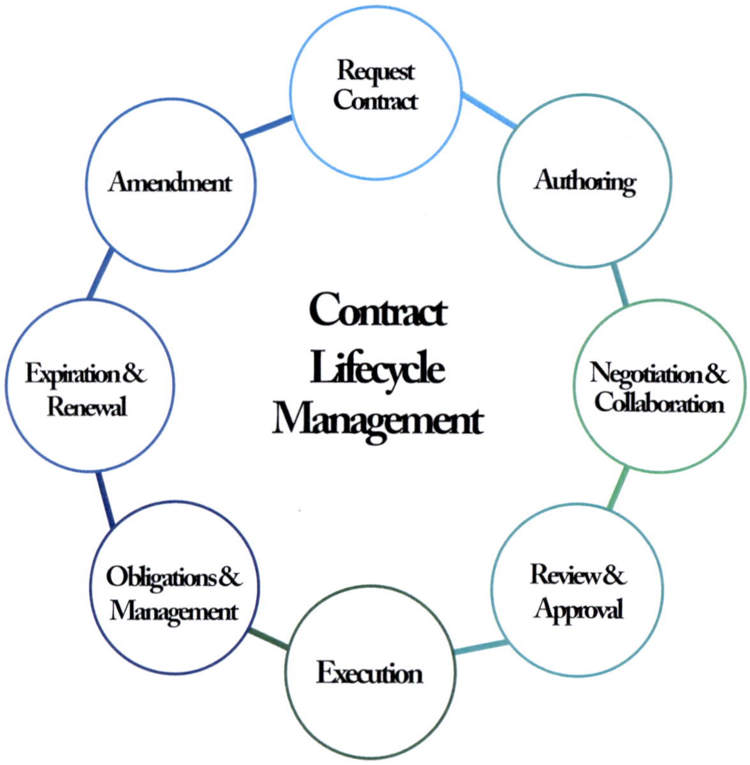

do or permit, or not to do. something expressed or implied by such agreement... A contract is an agreement to do or not to do a certain thing..."[3]

When entering written and binding contracts, make sure they are reviewed by your legal counsel. There is nothing worse than you and your business being bound to something that you had no intent to contract for. Contracts can be confusing, wrongly worded, contain conflicting language, and bind you and your business to a giant expensive legal headache that could take months or years to resolve and not necessarily in your favor. For example, in the law, it makes a big difference whether you agree to provide services at someone's "residence" or their "domicile." A "domicile" is a person's fixed, permanent, and principal home. A "residence" is a place where a person is dwelling. So if you agree to provide services to a person's residence, thinking of where their permanent domicile is (e.g., in Boston) you may be shocked to learn that their present residence is quite different (e.g., on the island of St. Thomas in the Caribbean).

Advantages of Long-Term Contracts

It depends whether your business is the performing or receiving party, and whether or not you are able to lock in favorable long-term pricing. Without a contract, or with a short-term contract, there is unpredictability and your clients can be easily lost due to competition. On the other hand, if you are the customer, a short-term contract can be advantageous if a lower price can be found when the contract terminates, or you can be stuck paying higher prices if market conditions change. Think of long and short-term contracts as hedging or a gamble. If you are the supplier, you want to lock clients into a contract at the highest fees the market will bear. If you are on the receiving end of

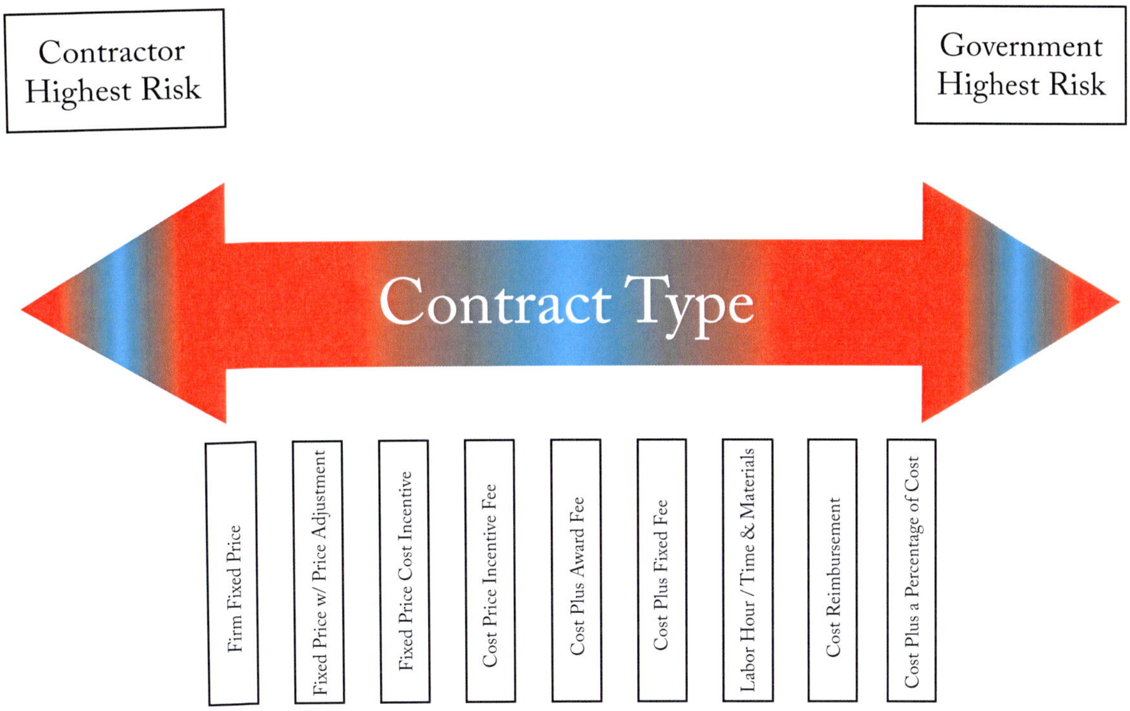

the contract, you want to lock in the lowest prices, while considering potential changing market conditions that could lower prices in the future. These are educated decisions that are made each and every day that will impact the profitability of your company.

Long term contracts provide predictability. A supplier can rely on the stability of revenue, and the recipient of goods and services can rely on the delivery of those goods and services in the contracted for timely manner. With all the business variables that can occur on a daily basis, it is comforting to know that you can rely on revenue and deliverables. Long term contracts provide for this stability. Also, the longer the term of the contracts, the longer time that exists for the businesses to renegotiate new contracts or renewals. These are the upsides to long term contracts; however, there are downsides.

Besides being locked in to terms that are no longer favorable, long term contracts have two other problematic issues to be aware of. The risk of breach of contract increases with the length of the contracts, making termination more likely if one side or the other is not meeting terms of the agreement. Remember, things change with time that will reflect certain standards and expectations. A contract can actually outdate itself. For example, what happens if parts or components are no longer made to produce an item, or if the technology contracted for is no longer the standard and becomes obsolete? Obviously, this will cause one side or the other desiring the contract to stop performing by necessity. Therefore, three years might be the maximum long-term contract that is feasible for a specific smartphone sale and purchase. If what was promised is not delivered, a *repudiation* or *breach* of contract can be acceptable and would hold up in a court of law. Another disadvantage to a long-term contract is the less chance available for any up-sells of goods or services. Psychologically, it is often very difficult to solicit changes with an already pre-existing client on a long-term contract.

The best advice when trying to decide who gets a long-term contract is to offer it strategically based upon the: product, service and market condition, and always as a goodwill and convenience factor to your existing clients with a history of repeated short-term agreements.[4]

Major Takeaway

Winning the contract game is all about leverage. When negotiating contracts, analyze leverage capabilities of all parties. Who has more leverage during the negotiation? Are the parties you are negotiating with aware of leverage or understand how to use leverage during contract negotiation? Make sure you do thorough research on the negotiation topic, the individuals taking part in the negotiation, the current position and pricing structure of the companies who you are negotiating with, and their competition. Figure out all the angles whereby the others in the negotiation perceive you to have the upper hand even when you don't. Always make the other party aware that, unlike most people, you are willing to walk away if things are not going in your direction. Willingness to walk away from negotiations is itself leverage.

Let's take a look at a very common contract transaction. Everyone chooses and uses hotels when they travel for business and for personal travel. Hotel expenses can be expensive and add up each year. When our firm negotiates hotel rates, we evaluate the industry. Are there loyalty and reward programs? If so, sign up for several hotel loyalty and reward programs in advance of any future travel. Also, sign up for credit cards and organizations that are affiliated with discounts at that hotel and offer hotel rewards points and cash reimbursements. Once you are all signed up for all these programs and you are ready to book your stay, you have all the leverage because barring a huge event at the location that you are booking, there will be more rooms available than will be sold. Hotels need to fill vacancies to pay overhead and rely on their food and beverage business to supplement their revenue stream. In the hotel business, it is always better for the hotel to have a room booked than to let it go vacant. Once you understand this, you are ready to negotiate.

Never make a reservation with the central reservation call center. Call the hotel directly where you want to stay. The corporate call center does not care about any individual hotel in their portfolio. Always speak to a person with authority to negotiate rates at the actual hotel front desk where you are booking. Most of the time they are franchised and not corporately owned. They care about their bottom line. Explain to the front desk why you are traveling, all your affiliations, that you are on a strict budget, and you are researching many hotel rates on line. At the same time, have your internet browsers open to all the hotel rates for your dates, then tell the hotel how much money you want to spend and ask them to search their system for the best rates and discount packages.

Be ready to calculate all the variables that you will be offered, in addition to the rate such as, free breakfast, free parking, free internet, and other perks that have value. During the writing of this book, I am actually in a hotel bar at 10:00 pm writing about this hotel booking experience. It went like this:

> Hello, my name is Lenny and I usually stay with the x-hotel chain. I am a rewards member of yours and have AAA and AARP. I am looking at your rates and your competitor's rates on the hotel websites and third-party web sites. Although I usually frequent hotel x, and they appear to be less expensive than your hotel online, I would prefer to stay with you as a change of pace and better location. Please provide your best price, any discounts, and any complimentary items such as a free breakfast or executive lounge access so that I can do my comparisons and hopefully book with you.

Remember, tell the reservation desk what you want to spend and all the free frills that will make you book, then ask them to do anything they can to match or beat your request. You will be surprised at the results. My results amounted to a 53% savings on a room night, free parking, free Wi-Fi, and two free breakfasts for me and my spouse ($40 + tax value). I use the hotel room reservation process as an example that everyone can relate to. Apply these same tactics and principles in all your contract negotiations for successful results.

References

1. *Sharpen Your Competitive Edge With These Futuristic SMB Tools*. Apr. 2018. URL: `https://www.inc.com/comcast/futuristic-technologies-your-business-should-use-now.html` (cited on page 91).
2. Ron Segura. *The Benefits of Long-Term Contracts*. May 2017. URL: `https://www.cmmonline.com/articles/the-benefits-of-long-term-contracts` (cited on page 91).
3. *contract*. In: *The Law Dictionary*. URL: `https://thelawdictionary.org/contract/` (cited on page 92).
4. Ben Barker. *The Pros and Cons of Multi-Year Client Contracts*. July 2015. URL: `https://www.continuum.net/blog/pros-and-cons-of-multi-year-client-contracts` (cited on page 93).

XII

Managing Risk Opportunistically

Overview

Irrespective of whatever else you are doing, keep in mind that the only two certainties in life are death and taxes. Everything else you do entails some degree of risk. There are no guarantees that you will wake up tomorrow morning. There are no guarantees that your bank will in fact pay you the correct interest that your funds on deposit should earn. There are no guarantees that the federal government will refund your overpaid taxes. There are no guarantees that a partner will live up to what your partner has promised. Everything has some degree of risk attached to it. But not all risks are equally likely, so you have to practice risk management.

What is *risk management*? It's a fancy way of saying, "reduce your chances of losing money, getting sued, etc." According to ISO 31000, the effect of uncertainty on objectives, Risk Management is defined as "the identification, evaluation, and prioritization of risks followed by coordinated and economical application of resources to minimize, monitor, and control the probability or impact of unfortunate events or to maximize the realization of opportunities."[1] Risk management's objective is to assure uncertainty does not deflect the endeavor from achieving its business goals.[2] It is good business practice to adhere to the ISO standards for the specific business industry.

ISO is a Geneva, Switzerland based nonprofit that sets standards that are used by over 160 nations. The standards that ISO sets cover a wide range of topics, from dates and times, to textiles (e.g., color fastness), steel (e.g., hardness), information technology (e.g., standards for CDs, DVDs, disk drives, etc.), light bulbs (e.g., screw width and pitch), and literally thousands of products and processes.

Logo of International Organization for Standardization. Image sourced from Wikipedia.[3]

Insurance

Why do we discuss risk management in business and why is it so important? Let's think of it this way, as an individual going about your normal day, you are managing risk constantly. Some risks you manage voluntarily, and some are mandated by some government. Some examples of individual risks that are managed voluntarily are health, life, disability insurances, and homeowner's insurance. In these instances, you are managing your risk with insurance premiums that will pay a monetary benefit to help financially if something goes wrong with your health. If a person has a heart attack with no health insurance coverage, they can be out of pocket for over a hundred thousand dollars for life saving treatment. On the other hand, a person covered by health insurance might only have to pay a $1000 deductible for the same treatment. With insurance, the risk is managed to the certainty of a $1000 deductible payment as opposed to the uncertainty of possible personal bankruptcy. This same principle holds true when owning a home. If you don't have homeowner's insurance that covers fire, and if there is a fire that burnt down your home, you lose your home. However, if you do have homeowner's insurance, the insurance company will provide the replacement value money to rebuild your home. This example illustrates how important risk management is, and why in some cases it is mandated by a government.

The perfect illustrative example of mandated individual risk management is automobile insurance. The reason why car insurance is mandated in order to maintain a driver's license is to cover or manage your risk of a car accident and injuring others. This point cannot be understated. For example, how is a $100,000 hospital and doctor bill going to be paid by someone who is at fault in a car accident and has only $1000 in assets and lives pay check to pay check? Because of the government mandated car insurance, the insurance company will pay all of the bills. These are prime examples of how you spread out and minimize your risk every day in the course of your individual routine, and things work pretty well.

Now that you understand how managing risk works, let's translate these same principles to your business. The trick is to act as if every transaction were going to be litigated. Choose your words and actions carefully and keep impeccable records; including logs of names, dates and discussions. This will create a record in the event there are any disputes. When you are contemplating starting a business, and before you start that business you should have a business plan that addresses risk management. Risk in business involves legal issues, financial matters, business decisions, and protection from these potential pitfalls. This is why you and your business want to have a risk management team of at least an attorney, accountant, consultant, and insurance broker. Confidentially share with them what you are setting out to do, so you are certain that any risks moving forward are managed. You want to avoid the risk of any improper choices when setting up your business from legal and accounting standpoints. You also want to make sure your business is covered from day one. To stress the importance of business insurance, we will address a few mock situations:

- What happens on day one of your new business when a customer slips and falls on your property
- You get into a car accident with your client in the car
- You act negligently

These are all reasons that demonstrate the importance of completely managing your risk when entering business ownership. Remember, different types of businesses will determine different types of insurances and policies. There is a market for every type of insurance; even weather. Let's say you own a rock music band and your outdoor concert is rained out, canceled, and refunds given to all the spectators; you could have bought concert cancellation insurance that covered weather. If you did purchase that kind of insurance policy protection, you could be paid a covered benefit of your lost profits, in the form of refunding the cost to rent the facility and the refund price of every ticket that had to be refunded due to the cancellation and non-rescheduling of the event. We used insurance of risk as an example in order to provide some insight and an oversimplified way to look at, while being able to relate to risk management.

Walling Off Risks

Consulting with your lawyer about the risks you and your firm are facing is always a good idea. Consider two examples. First, contracts get canceled all the time. Sometimes they get canceled for reasons beyond anybody's control (often called force majeure, meaning acts of god, such as flooding from a storm, a wildfire that spreads, or a union strike). But, it often happens that the other party cancels out because it is no longer economically desirable for the other party to live up to the expectations held for it. If such an action would materially affect your firm, when you draft the contract, insert language such that if the other party fails to live up to the contract, or if delivery of results occurs later than the date agreed upon, the other party has to pay a penalty.

Second, our experiences with many entrepreneurs is that many run several businesses simultaneously. For example, one entrepreneur runs a lawn and garden business and also runs an interior decoration business. Another designs web sites and separately runs a business that assists businesses with their marketing endeavors. Such multi-businesses are commendable, as long as each business is separately incorporated (or run as separate LLCs). Because, if litigation arises, and your firm is run as one giant entity, the plaintiff will try to collect damages all of your businesses. Your lawn and garden business may be running at break even, while your interior design business is flourishing. Even if the litigation arose because of the lawn and garden business, the plaintiff will try to collect from your profits in interior design.

Keeping a legal fence between your various businesses protects earnings in all your other

businesses from the one that is being sued.

Clearly, risk management is complicated with many complex facets to consider for all businesses. In order to develop a solid risk management plan, the risks must be identified using proven methods. These methods consist of the following elements that should be performed, in the following order:

1. Identify and characterize threats.
2. Assess the vulnerability of critical assets to specific threats.
3. Determine the risk (i.e. the expected likelihood and consequences of specific types of attacks on specific assets) and identify ways to control those risks.
4. Review controls and prioritize risk reduction measures.

Once you have used all the methods to identify risks, then certain principles should be applied as the business standard to manage the major and/or most likely risks that you and your firm are facing. The International Organization for Standardization (ISO) identifies the following principles of risk management that should be incorporated into your thinking:[4]

- Create value – resources expended to mitigate risk should be less than the consequence of inaction.
- Be an integral part of organizational processes.
- Be part of decision making process.
- Explicitly address uncertainty and assumptions.
- Be a systematic and structured process.
- Be based on the best available information.
- Be tailorable.
- Take human factors into account.
- Be transparent and inclusive.
- Be dynamic, iterative and responsive to change.
- Be capable of continual improvement and enhancement.
- Be continually or periodically re-assessed.

Once the business has a risk management assessment plan that has followed the ISO methods and principles, it is time to "Prepare a Risk Treatment Plan", which should document the decisions about how each of the identified risks should be managed. Mitigation of risks often means selection of security controls, which should be documented in a Statement of Applicability that identifies which particular control objectives and controls from the standard have been selected, and why."[5]

Major Takeaway

A business must manage its risk, but not all risks. The risks to be managed are the major ones facing the firm (if one of those risks were to occur, it would have a devastating impact on the firm) and the ones the firm is most likely to encounter. Although is it possible that a meteor could fall on your head, it is such a remote risk that is probably not worth worrying about. Market-changing innovations and competition itself are very important risks to manage. Know the marketplace and your competitors and likely competitors intimately, and be ready to forecast and predict the future based on competitive behavior and consumer trends. "It can be hard for some to imagine now, but there was a time when video rental stores like Blockbuster Video were a regular part of your weekend plans. Online video streaming services such as Netflix and small kiosk-based rental systems such as Redbox destroyed the old video rental business model. Blockbuster came to the party late, even though it got an early invite. In 2000, Netflix proposed that it would handle Blockbuster's online component, and Blockbuster could host its in-store component (thus eliminating the need for mailed DVDs). According to an interview with former Netflix CFO Barry McCarthy, "They just about laughed us out of their office." Blockbuster went belly up and Netflix went on to thrive. And since Netflix is behind such shows as House of Cards, Orange is the New Black, and Daredevil, one could argue the world is a better place because of Blockbuster's blunder."[6]

Also, minimize risk with a good quality assurance risk management protocol; check and double check. "Decimals and fractions cause headaches for many school children, and once, they even stymied some of the greatest minds in the country. In 1999, a Mars orbiter that Lockheed Martin designed for NASA was lost in space due to a simple error where the engineers at Lockheed used English measurements while the NASA team used metric ones. The mismatch led to a formation on the $125 million craft malfunctioning and the probe being lost. Though it was unusual for Lockheed to use English measurements for a NASA design (since NASA has stipulated using metric measures for many years), there were still numerous occasions where the error should have been caught and wasn't."[6]

Our consulting firm was hired to protect a lucrative contract and promised series of purchase orders from a subcontractor hired by a contractor to deliver technology to a very important company in the aerospace industry. For some unexplained reason, the subcontractor point person continually delayed purchase orders that should have been approved per standard operating procedure and protocol. Any substantial delays could result in penalty clauses to be invoked up the line that could have financially negatively impacted our client. We were consulting with our client from the project inception, gathered the records, presented them to the Vice President of the contracting company, and our client was granted an in perpetuity, noncancellable purchase order with a sum certain guaranteed payment. The rest of the project was completed without delay and all involved were grateful for the successful timely outcome.

References

1. Douglas W. Hubbard. *The failure of risk management: why its broken and how to fix it*. Wiley, 2009, page 46 (cited on page 99).
2. Ricardo Antunes and Vicente Gonzalez. "A Production Model for Construction: A Theoretical Framework". In: *Buildings* 5.1 (2015), pages 209–228. DOI: 10.3390/buildings5010209 (cited on page 99).
3. Wikimedia Commons. *File:ISO Logo (Red square).svg — Wikimedia Commons, the free media repository*. [Online; accessed 5-April-2021]. 2021. URL: https://commons.wikimedia.org/w/index.php?title=File:ISO_Logo_(Red_square).svg&oldid=528893786 (cited on page 99).
4. *Risk management — Guidelines*. Standard. Geneva, CH: International Organization for Standardization, Mar. 2018 (cited on page 102).
5. *Information technology — Security techniques — Information security management systems — Requirements TECHNICAL CORRIGENDUM 2*. Standard. Geneva, CH: International Organization for Standardization, Dec. 2015 (cited on page 103).
6. Peter Roesler. *8 of the Biggest Business Mistakes in History*. Apr. 2015. URL: https://www.inc.com/peter-roesler/8-of-the-biggest-business-mistakes-in-history.html (cited on page 103).

XIII

Opportunities From Consolidation

Goals of Business Consolidation

According to the dictionary by Merriam-Webster, *consolidate* is defined:

1. To bring together (separate parts) into a single or unified whole; unite; combine.
2. To discard the unused or unwanted items of and organize the remaining.
3. To make solid or firm; solidify; strengthen.

Business consolidation involves transitioning more than one business unit, company, location or department into one. The purposes and ultimate goals of consolidation are to improve efficiency, market share, and save money in the long run by:

- Eliminating redundant personnel.
- Reducing duplicate processes.
- Reducing locations.
- Combining separate entities into one larger legal entity.

Successful consolidation also improves communications since there are fewer people involved, fewer organizational layers to cope with, and fewer locations to span. Successful consolidations reduce the time needed to introduce new procedures, new processes, and new technologies. It is easier to train fewer people, and it is easier to implement change.

Types of Consolidation

Once a business has chosen to consolidate, there are several ways to consolidate. Consolidation options can include: statutory consolidation, statutory merger, stock acquisition, and variable interest entity options. When a brand-new entity that never existed before is formed from multiple entities that no longer will exist, a "statutory consolidation" has taken place. (In 1901, Carnegie Steel Company, Federal Steel Company, National Steel Company and J.P. Morgan consolidated into the new entity United States Steel).

A *statutory merger* results from the acquisition of a company that is then completely liquidated of its assets, while incorporating or dismantling its operations, and will still operate under the name

and brand of the entity that did the acquiring (Merck acquires Schering Plough and renames Merck). When both companies survive in name and/or brand after one company purchases more than 50% of another is known as a "stock acquisition" (Time Inc. and Warner Communications resulted in Time Warner).

Variable interest entities (VIE) are formed by equity firms as investors with or without voting rights. These equity firms purchase the private or publicly traded companies, leave the company intact, and act as solely an investor in the transaction (equity firm Apollo Global Management LLC purchases Fresh Market and ADT, etc.) The variable interest entity owns a controlling interest in the business that is not based on a majority of its voting rights. There are major advantages to consolidations. These advantages include:

- Less expensive financing interest rates
- Better business stability
- Reduction of competitors
- Lower overhead
- Increased profits
- More assets
- More negotiating leverage for lower cost supplies
- Concentration of market share
- Enhanced expansive product line-up and revenue streams
- Attracting a more skilled staff
- Larger demographic and geographic regions
- Economies of scale
- Larger customer base.

However, consolidation is not cost free. Downsides include potential culture clash with reduced flexibility, integration failure, and short-term higher expenses in order to consolidate. The reason firms merge with competitors is to improve a firm's strategic position within a single industry; this is known as horizontal integration. "If the target firm is more valuable inside the acquiring firm than as a continued standalone company," then firms should pursue horizontal integration. "This implies that the net value creation of a horizontal acquisition must be positive to aid in gaining and sustaining competitive advantage. An industry-wide trend toward horizontal integration leads to industry consolidation." "The wave of recent horizontal integration in the U.S. airline industry, for example, provided several benefits to the surviving carriers. By reducing excess capacity, the mergers between Delta and Northwest Airlines, United Airlines and Continental, Southwest and AirTran, and American and US Airways lowered competitive intensity in the industry overall."[1] Having fewer competitors will equate to higher industry profitability within that company.

Managing Consolidation

No matter when you choose to consolidate or how you choose to consolidate, "...ensure a smooth transition – and make sure that every business process works during and after re-structuring... For some companies, the acquisitions happened years ago and the enterprise has been living with the pain and expense of a tangle of diverse systems for a long time. Maybe it's time to untangle, streamline, and consolidate your enterprise application landscape. For many firms, today's pace of change is making maintenance and upgrades a real challenge, so for them the choice to consolidate is clear."[2]

With that being said, the reason high-performing companies are so driven on efficient consolidation is because of management, shareholders, and stakeholders demanding immediate information and quick results. According to Ernst & Young, "Today's CFOs are under pressure to report accurately, quickly and more often to management and stakeholders. At the same time, they are expected to act as a business partner and provide pro-active support for senior management's decision making. Their role and the demands placed on them continues to evolve and shift. Consolidation and consolidated financial reporting can improve a finance department's efficiency and effectiveness, helping CFOs address the challenge of meeting increasing requirements with often-limited resources... The current economic climate has also caused many companies to change in size or to enter new markets in order to remain competitive. In all these cases, consolidation and reporting form an integral part of effective management and are key to providing accurate information to investors and regulators in an evolving environment."[3]

If your business is looking to improve your consolidation and reporting process, Ernst & Young identifies 10 reasons that include:[3]

1. Improve the quality of the reporting packages sent by local entities.
2. Save time on your intercompany reconciliation process.
3. Reduce manual consolidation entries.
4. Shorten the control activities of the consolidation process performed by the central team.
5. Obtain final reports directly from system outputs.
6. Integrate new entities without putting the whole process at risk.
7. Reduce dependence on specific individuals while creating a way to share knowledge and document the consolidation process.
8. Update IT reporting tools to account for new analyses or GAAP requirements.
9. Coordinate or merge your business and financial consolidation processes.
10. Optimize resources and reduce costs.

Consolidation should result in: standardized platforms, efficient financial systems and processes, accelerated productivity, cost containment, and operating within budget to be successful. In addition, business execution must be seamless during all consolidation steps and functions – "Smooth, continuous business operations – and no delays because of IT system failures or glitches."[2] Seamless business integration and continuity are the objectives. "Consolidations can bring an enormous number of application changes – removing, adding, and restructuring business processes, transferring data, changing interfaces, and introducing new applications for parts of the business....Consolidations impact technology, IT infrastructure and business applications – which can introduce risk to your business process continuity. Automation can help ensure success on the IT side for large and small enterprise system consolidations..."[2]

Accurate reports, analysis, forecasts, and ideal operations are mandatory. Therefore, introducing as much automation as possible "...can help ensure success on the IT side for large and small enterprise system consolidations... Functional test automation platforms like Worksoft Certify® can be used to validate that processes are executed with the highest quality – before, during, and after the project. After all, business operations can't stop because you are in the midst of a reorganization..."[2] Consolidation must be as rapid as possible, adhering to a very strict timeline without disrupting the company's business operations. Business users should not even be aware of restructuring.

Ideally, companies prefer to test automation during consolidations. Most businesses undergoing consolidation want to:

- Achieve seamless consolidation and reduce business disruption.
- Achieve quality core business process execution during and after consolidation.
- Achieve validation of business processes which involve multiple platforms, interfaces, locations, and devices

- Achieve error mitigation avoiding production errors before they impact the business.
- Achieve consolidation time and cost reductions.
- Achieve a successful consolidation using standard technology integration.

Data on Mergers and Acquisitions

Remember, you are pursuing merger, acquisition, and consolidation success. So, how many mergers and acquisitions succeed and how many of them fail? What is the definition of success or failure when related to the outcomes of mergers and acquisition? Is it successful because you eliminated your competition although the revenues suffered? Is it a success because you won the "bidding war" and now own an overvalued company? Is it a success because you now own the company you always admired, regardless of weak financials or purposely overlooked faults? Remember the old adage, "love is blind." By briefly exploring the merger and acquisition "failures" and their statistics, hopefully, you will learn not to make the same mistakes.

There were $1.5 trillion worth of mergers and acquisitions in 2016.[4] The most difficult and complex aspect of a corporate merger and acquisition deal is the integration of the companies and its employees. It is this integration process, that leads to the highest rate of merger and acquisition failures. Many studies have been done by M & A business team experts: Gerds and Schewe; Chang, Curtis, and Jenk; Watkins and Copley; and KPMG that demonstrate between a 50%-70% failure rate of all merger and acquisitions.[5,6,7,8] As was eluded to earlier, it is the human characteristic's integration of employee "corporate": cultural differences, politics, and miscommunications, that is the greatest cause of failure, followed by bad business strategies. More specifically, M & A Study researchers have shown that international mergers, such as by telecommunications companies have the highest M & A failure rates with the lowest shareholder value returns. It is further shown that two-thirds of the M & A failures are because the companies ignored the employees input and feedback; leading to quitting, absenteeism, disloyalty, lack of motivation, or sabotage.[9]

As you can see, there is a wide variation of success or failure of a M&A. This variation is due to different definitions of success or failure ranging from internal strife and discontent to external shareholder value, and everything in between.

Therefore, the best advice, when considering a merger and acquisition, is to create your team, clearly define all the goals, communicate like crazy so everyone knows what to expect and what exactly is expected from them. do everything else possible to attain those defined goals, then define your success or failure based on your team's definitive goal criteria. With so many variables and unforeseeable possible issues, the outcome will never result in 100% perfection or in being able to satisfy all those involved.

Major Takeaway

There are many good reasons to consolidate. Note that any costs that can be cut, flow directly to the bottom line. Note that a simpler firm is easier to manage. Note that in a simpler firm it is easier to introduce change and to get that change adopted faster.

However, to achieve the benefits of consolidation, the process of undertaking consolidation must be managed carefully. In general, your biggest problems will stem from your personnel. Over time, many people get comfortable with the status quo ante—they understand their coworkers, they have figured out how to deal with their boss, they know organizational routines, and they know what to expect on a daily basis. Change threatens to upset all that history and knowledge and to introduce many unknowns. Communicate often and openly. Spot fear and deal with it; reassure everyone that they will master the present unknowns and will be better off afterwards.

Merger and consolidation failures are too common but they can be minimized. After the 2005 Sprint Nextel $35 billion "merger of equals" deal, the leadership of the two companies realized that the two companies proved too difficult to "integrate."

Sprint Nextel shut down the "Nextel network" in 2013. This is a prime example demonstrating the importance of full integration due diligence. Before the consolidation, the two companies should have tested the integration capability to prove the technology will work. This way, before moving further and closing the deal the two companies would have realized integration would not be possible, instead of losing $30 billion. Sometimes no deal is the best deal.

Another consolidation failure involved two of the largest competing railroads in history. Not researching the future travel industry, the $4.6 billion Pennsylvania and New York Central Railroad Companies merged in 1968. Two years later the firm was bankrupt. If the railroad companies did proper due diligence and were properly guided with effective leadership, they could have merged and also diversified by adding commercial capability and acquiring or merging with an airline or road construction company.[10]

References

1. Frank T. Rothaermel. *Strategic management: concepts*. McGraw-Hill Irwin, 2019 (cited on page 108).
2. Brian Smith. *One Business, Many Systems? Time to Consolidate!* Feb. 2016. URL: https://www.cio.com/article/3034231/data-center/one-business-many-systems-time-to-consolidate.html (cited on page 109).
3. Thierry Cornille and Laure Deshayes. *Consolidation and reporting: Improving processes for faster financial reporting of multiple entities*. Ernst & Young, 2016. URL: https://www.ey.com/Publication/vwLUAssets/EMEIA_FAAS_Consolidation_Reporting/%24File/EMEIA_FAAS_Consolidation_Reporting.pdf (cited on page 109).

4. *Global M&A Review 2017*. Bureau Van Dijk: A Moody's Analytics Company, 2017. URL: https://www.bvdinfo.com/BvD/media/reports/Global-2017.pdf (cited on page 110).

5. Johannes Gerds and Gerhard Schewe. *Post Merger integration Unternehmenserfolg durch Integration Excellence*. Springer Gabler, 2014 (cited on page 110).

6. R.A. Chang, G.A. Curtis, and J. Jenk. *Keys to the kingdom: How an integrated IT capability can increase your odds of M&A success*. Accenture, 2002 (cited on page 110).

7. A. Watkins and S. Copley. *Operational and IT due diligence*. 2004. URL: http://www.pwchk.com/home/eng/oprisk.html (cited on page 110).

8. Han Nguyen and Brian H. Kleiner. "The effective management of mergers". In: *Leadership & Organization Development Journal* 24.8 (2003), pages 447–454. DOI: 10.1108/01437730310505876 (cited on page 110).

9. Godfred Koi-Akrofi. "Mergers and Acquisitions failure rates and perspectives on why they fail". In: *International Journal of Innovation and Applied Studies* 17 (July 2016), pages 150–158 (cited on page 110).

10. Oct. 2018. URL: http://www.cbinsights.com/research/merger-acquisition-corporate-fails/ (cited on page 111).

XIV

Opportunities To Merge With/Acquire Another Company

Why do it?

According to the Merriam-Webster dictionary, *merge* is defined as:

1. To cause to combine or coalesce; unite.
2. To combine, blend, or unite gradually so as to blur the individuality or individual identity of.

Acquire is defined as:

1. To come into possession or ownership of; get as one's own.
2. To gain for oneself through one's actions or efforts.

Mergers and acquisitions can be very rewarding and the correct strategy in many instances. Sometimes, you are in control of the decision to merge or to acquire another company, and sometimes economic or industry forces could control your merger or acquisition decision. When considering mergers or acquisitions, it is important to understand the transactions and how the businesses could be affected on many levels: legal structure, accounting liabilities, tax consequences, and transaction costs. "Mergers and acquisitions (M&A) refers to the consolidation of companies or assets. M&A can include a number of different transactions, such as: mergers, acquisitions, consolidations, tender offers, purchase of assets, and management acquisitions."[1]

Questions to be answered before consolidating companies are: Is it best to merge with another company or outright acquire it? In addition, is the planned result of consolidation for: synergy, diversification, growth, lower cost wholesale and supplier pricing, to eliminate competition, or a combination thereof?

Some mergers will seek *synergy*, where two or more organizations can accomplish more together than separately; and/or in order to achieve higher revenues, lower costs, and better performance by combining the best attributes of both companies and eliminating weaknesses. Other mergers seek diversity. By diversifying a business, the plan is to maximize profits in good times and manage the risk of losses during bad times if there is a down turn in the other business sector.

Mergers and acquisitions should only be undertaken when they yield healthy growth with increased market share. Why else would you decide to merge or acquire? Growth and stability of the business must be a main factor. A successful acquisition can expand a company's market presence, improving profitability, and filling in the gaps in a company's product or service portfolio, and help other performance metrics.[4]

A horizontal merger of like companies, for the right price, can increase your market share immediately, with little or no effort. Another merger and acquisition option is the vertical merger. Vertical mergers or acquisitions will increase the industry value chain through supply chain buying power and lower supply costs by eliminating supplier profit margins. Plus, you now own a supplier company or distributor within your industry, minimizing supply problems, while owning an additional profit center.

Another strategy for success through the merger and acquisition process is elimination of the competition. Why compete with a competitor if you can buy and own them? Want to resolve the "competition" problem? Buy them. In other words, "if you can't beat them, join them", or eliminate them from the marketplace. Now, you have a bigger and stronger company without the headache of competition and price constraints. A buyout of another business could allow you to immediately raise prices to recoup the cost of the company purchase. As you can see, it is worthwhile to always keep an eye out for merger and acquisition opportunities.

MERGER	ACQUISITION
Merger refers to consolidation of two or more companies to form an all-new entity with a new name. Merger assists the companies in uniting their strengths, resources, and weaknesses. Mergers lead to a reduction in trade barriers and competition.	Acquisition is the purchase of an entity by another entity. This can be done either by acquiring ownership over 51% of its share capital or by taking over the assets of the company. The acquiring company is more influential in terms of structure, operations, size when compared to the target company.
Types of Mergers	**Types of Acquisitions**
• Horizontal • Vertical • Congeneric • Reverse • Conglomerate	• Hostile • Friendly • Buyout

Comparison between mergers and acquisitions.[2,3]

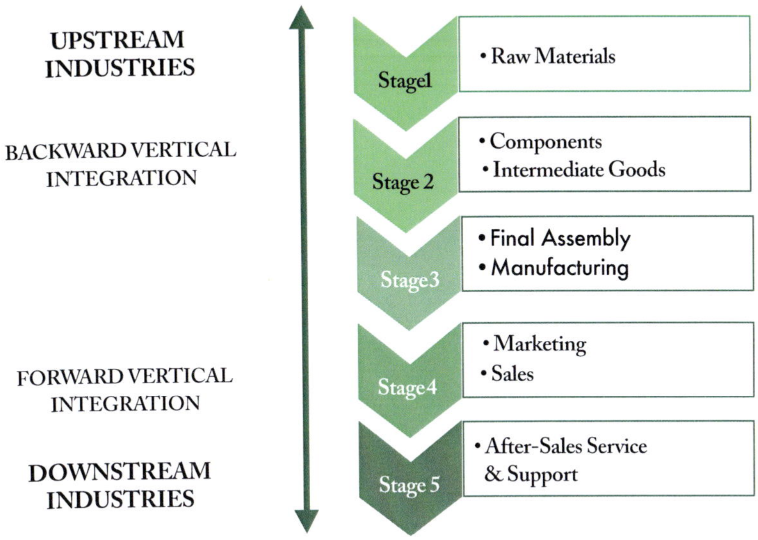

Backward and forward vertical integration along an industry value chain.[5]

> *CAVEAT*: If your firm is big enough, the government make block the merger or acquisition. As a matter of public policy, people want fair competition, not monopoly-like competition, where just a few firms dictate prices or features. Thus, the federal government has blocked proposed mergers between Sprint and T-Mobile, ensuring that there are four major telecommunication companies (the other two being AT&T and Verizon). Similarly, the four major air transport firms (American Airlines, Delta, Southwest, and United) have never attempted a merger or acquisition, knowing that the government would block it.

Due Diligence

When one business is ready to merge with, or acquire the other business, *timing* and *due diligence* are important to identify all liabilities, filtering out potential risks and valuation considerations, assess the probability of the risk's occurrence, that there are no outstanding taxes owed, and the "tax basis" is most favorable. In other words, do not enter a deal until the entire transaction is reviewed by qualified lawyers, accountants, and business consultants. These professionals will help guide you in determining whether it is best to solely buy the assets, without buying "the business." When acquiring another business, demand a "clearance letter" from all the taxing authorities to confirm all taxes are paid to date and there will be no outstanding taxes that could become your responsibility after the deal is "closed." Accounts payable and receivables are important issues. If you will be taking over any of these accounts, make sure it is reflected in the purchase price and agree on who will be paying or collecting these receivables. If there is an existing lease for the business that is being acquired:

1. Get a copy.

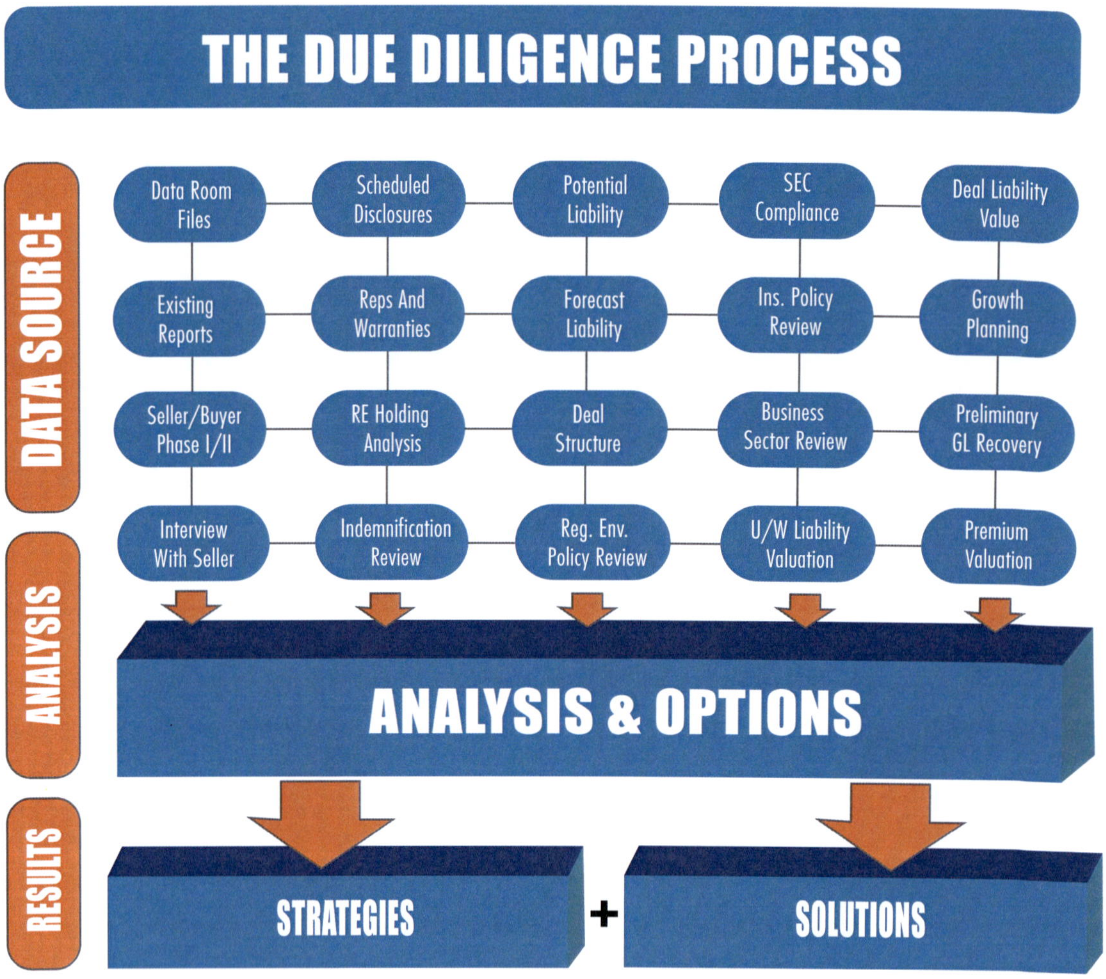
THE DUE DILIGENCE PROCESS
DATA SOURCE
ANALYSIS
RESULTS
Data Room Files
Scheduled Disclosures
Potential Liability
SEC Compliance
Deal Liability Value
Existing Reports
Reps And Warranties
Forecast Liability
Ins. Policy Review
Growth Planning
Seller/Buyer Phase I/II
RE Holding Analysis
Deal Structure
Business Sector Review
Preliminary GL Recovery
Interview With Seller
Indemnification Review
Reg. Env. Policy Review
U/W Liability Valuation
Premium Valuation
ANALYSIS & OPTIONS
STRATEGIES
+
SOLUTIONS

2. Read and understand the terms.
3. Make sure the purchase price reflects the lease asset of the business that is being purchased.

Quite frankly, a business could be worth considerably less if there are less than 2 years on a lease without a renewable option. The business could be extremely location sensitive. Meet with the landlord, assume the existing lease, and/or negotiate new lease terms that will only be binding if the business acquisition goes through. Also, any security deposits on an assumed lease might need to be reflected in the purchase price. Determine whether there are any pre-paid expenses that you will be assuming, such as pre-paid advertising or inventory.

Again, this is all negotiated in the purchase offer, therefore this information must be known by the purchaser. To save money, and get the deal right the first time, negotiate and agree to a non-binding a letter of intent. This is a crucial step to outline all of the terms of the buy/sell transaction before lawyers start billing for time to draft the final agreements. As part of this letter of intent, the purchaser might want to require an "indemnity clause" that can hold the purchaser harmless for acts that took place before the sale. "Good will" is an important aspect of any business asset. The sellers are an integral part of the business, so make sure the seller remains on premises for a negotiated amount of time as part of the purchase in order to introduce the buyers to customers, suppliers, and employees. If more than the negotiated "good will" time is necessary, have a negotiated consultant fee and added time agreed to for this additional transition time.

Finally, know who the employees are of the company that is being purchased.

> "Put a provision in the sales contract that reads as follows: 'Seller and Buyer will announce the proposed sale to all employees of the Business within forty-eight hours before the closing, and Buyer will be given a reasonable opportunity to meet with each employee individually before the closing date to determine, to Buyer's reasonable satisfaction, the employee's willingness to continue working for the Business.' Then add a provision allowing you to walk from the deal if you're not totally satisfied that the key employees will stay on board at least long enough for you to learn what they already know."[6]

When the opportunity to acquire or merge a business arises, consideration should be given to the new entity's: brand messaging; assets, liabilities, revenues, and profits; agreement not to compete; cash flow and cost of running the business; culture similarities; legal environment; risk management; competition and market share; aligned values; identification and creation of new value.[7]

As you get closer to finalizing the deal, ask yourself, what am I actually acquiring? If it is customers, get a list of the major customers and get permission to approach a few of them (you chose the ones, NOT the company being acquired). Tell those customers that you are conducting research for the firm and ask them what they like about the firm, its products, its services, its personnel, its technology, etc., and what they don't like about it.

Similarly, if you are primarily acquiring talent, get permission to sit down with a set of the key people you wish to keep on. Learn their thinking. What is the firm slow to capitalize upon? What opportunities are they missing? If they were running the firm, what would they do differently? What other firms in the industry do they admire, and why? Is there a star player out there that they would like to see on their team?

And, if it is equipment, technology, or location that is the main driver, hire appropriately knowledgeable consultants to come in an assess those elements. Are each of those ideal, cutting edge, or otherwise best in class? What changes would those consultants recommend?

Data

The sad fact is that many mergers and acquisitions fail to attain the objectives set for them. Some studies report 50% failure rates, others 90%, but the majority of studies, and the generally agreed upon consensus is that 70% of mergers and acquisitions don't live up to their promise.[8]

There are many reasons for this common failure. Without sufficient due diligence up front, there are often post-merger unpleasant surprises – key players leave, customers bolt, systems are discovered to not work as promised, etc. Sometimes when it becomes known that company A is trying to buy firm X, other bidders (B, C, D, ...) step in and make counteroffers—driving the acquisition price up. Sometimes the target firm, X, does not wish to be taken over or believes the price offered is too low—this also leads to having to pay more for the target firm. Smart buyers go into an acquisition with a maximum price that they will pay for the target firm. If the target firm's price rises, for whatever reason, smart buyers walk away form it and look for another candidate.

Unfortunately, some buyers fall in love with the target firm (don't forget that love is blind) and pay whatever it takes to get the firm. (And like some lovesick drunks, they wake up the next morning and ask themselves what they just did.) Finally, post-acquisition, some buyers learn of substantial problems with the firm they just bought, and significant cash infusions are necessary to make the deal work. But some deals just don't work, causing buyer to throw good money after bad to try to convince others that the deal was masterful. Look at the lessons from the Vietnam War. Several presidents in a row knew that the war was unwinnable, yet they kept sending troops, arms, and aid to ensure that they were not tagged as the first US president to lose a war.

Major Takeaway

M&A is a fun topic to observe. Many companies you are familiar with, or are customers of, were created from mergers & acquisitions. So, what makes large companies merge or get bought out? A lot can be learned from the posturing, decision making, and the process of multi-billion dollar companies being merged or acquired; especially when you have done business with, or are customers of those companies and have experience with their brands. Some mergers or acquisitions are brilliant, and some are disasters. Even the smartest people make stupid mistakes. Learn and do not repeat these consolidation errors.

The Worst M&A To Date:

The AOL Time Warner merger in 2001, worth $111 billion dollars, was one of the worst deals in business history. In 2009, they broke up, with a loss to shareholders of $200 billion. Imagine a traditional mature entertainment and communications company that began in 1923 merging with an immature teenager, AOL, that started doing business in 1985. The terms of the deal called for AOL shareholders to own 55% of the new, combined company.

It is widely speculated that Steve Case double talked and hyped technology and duped Time Warner into acquiring a business they knew nothing about. "It was clear to insiders that the culture clash between the two would prove to be insurmountable."[9] "A few scant months after the deal closed, the dot com bubble burst and the economy went into recession. Advertising dollars evaporated, and AOL was forced to take a goodwill write-off of nearly $99 billion in 2002, an astonishing sum that shook even the business-hardened writers of the Wall Street Journal. AOL was also losing subscribers and subscription revenue. The total value of AOL stock subsequently went from $226 billion to about $20 billion."[10]

In 2015, Verizon bought AOL for $4.4 billion. This Acquisition by AOL and merger of Time Warner is a prime example of not knowing each other's business and the business environment. The two companies combined were not able to do what they did best separately. The failure of the AOL-Time Warner merger is the subject of a book by Nina Munk entitled Fools Rush In: Steve Case, Jerry Levin, and the Unmaking of AOL Time Warner (2005). Other bad merger deals were Daimler and Chrysler, Mattel and the Learning Company, Sears and K Mart, Quaker Oats and Snapple, Vodafone and Mannesmann, RFS Holdings and ABN AMRO, and Sprint and Nextel.

One of the best M & A deals was Exxon and Mobil in 1999 forming Exxon Mobil, the largest oil company in the world. This was an interesting horizontal merger of two companies that were together in the past "...it reunited its 19th Century former selves — John D. Rockefeller's Standard Oil Company of New Jersey (Exxon) and Standard Oil Company of New York (Mobil)."[11] In order to make the merger work, Exxon Mobil had to shed some gas station locations to avoid anti-trust behavior that would prevent the merger. Other very successful mergers were: Disney and Pixar, Sirius and XM Radio, AT&T and Bell South, Warner Lambert and Pfizer, SAB Miller and Anheuser-Busch InBev, and Dow and DuPont.

Bottom line, most mergers and acquisitions subtract from the shareholder value of acquiring firms and add shareholder value to the acquired firms. Therefore, buyer and shareholder beware of whether you are on the side of the acquirer or acquiree in any acquisition.

References

1. Will Kenton. *Mergers and Acquisitions - M&A*. May 2018. URL: `www.investopedia.com/terms/m/mergersandacquisitions.asp` (cited on page 115).
2. Christina Majaski. *What Is the Difference Between Mergers and Acquisitions?* Oct. 2020. URL: `https://www.investopedia.com/ask/answers/021815/what-difference-between-merger-and-acquisition.asp` (cited on page 116).
3. Surbhi S. *Difference Between Merger and Acquisition*. July 2018. URL: `https://keydifferences.com/difference-between-merger-and-acquisition.html#ixzz4tEYYMWTI` (cited on page 116).
4. *Mergers and Acquisitions due diligence | Deloitte US | Center for Board Effectiveness*. July 2017. URL: `https://www2.deloitte.com/us/en/pages/center-for-board-effectiveness/articles/the-intersection-of-due-diligence-and-governance.html` (cited on page 115).
5. Frank T. Rothaermel. *Strategic management: concepts*. McGraw-Hill Irwin, 2019 (cited on page 117).

6. Cliff Ennico. *10 Things to Look Out for When Buying a Business*. Nov. 2005. URL: https://www.entrepreneur.com/article/81176 (cited on page 119).

7. *10 Things to Look For When Considering an Acquisition*. Nov. 2017. URL: https://smallbiztrends.com/2015/05/considering-an-acquisition.html (cited on page 119).

8. Mitchell Lee Marks, Philip Mirvis, and Ron Ashkenas. "Surviving M&A". In: *Harvard Business Review* (2017): *March-April 2017*, pages 145–149 (cited on page 120).

9. *Final farewell to worst deal in history - AOL-Time Warner*. Nov. 2009. URL: https://www.telegraph.co.uk/finance/newsbysector/mediatechnologyandtelecoms/media/6622875/Final-farewell-to-worst-deal-in-history-AOL-Time-Warner.html (cited on page 121).

10. Rita Gunther McGrath. *15 years later, lessons from the failed AOL-Time Warner merger*. Jan. 2015. URL: http://fortune.com/2015/01/10/15-years-later-lessons-from-the-failed-aol-time-warner-merger/ (cited on page 121).

11. Jan. 2014. URL: https://www.cnbc.com/2009/12/29/Top-10-Best-(and-Worst)-Mergers-of-All-Time.html (cited on page 121).

XV

Is Now The Time To Add High Technology To My Business?

Low Technology and High Technology

According to the Merriam-Webster Dictionary, *technology* is:

- The branch of knowledge that deals with the creation and use of technical means and their interrelationship with life society and the environment, drawing upon such subjects as industrial arts, engineering, applied science, and pure science.
- The application of this knowledge for practical ends.
- The terminology of an art, science, etc.; technical nomenclature.

A distinction is often made between high tech and low tech applications. Low technology includes most tools that are familiar to you – a screwdriver, an electric motor, television, microwaves, etc. High technology usually consists of tools that have been developed recently—gene editing in biology, 3-D printing, solar cells, virtual reality, autonomous vehicles, etc. In many cases, when one "purchases" something that is high tech (e.g., a robot), what one actually purchases is the *right* to use the high technology, not the high technology "device" (product or service) itself. Consequently, in those cases where you only purchase the rights to use the high technology, you usually have to sign an end user license agreement (called a EULA) before you may use the device. Most EULAs are long, filled with legal jargon only understandable by another lawyer, and designed to protect the company, not you. In particular, most EULAs stipulate that you do not own the device, you may only use it for the intended purpose, you may not sell or assign the rights, and if anything goes wrong, the company is held harmless (and in many cases you are forbidden to sue the company and may only take your case to a company appointed arbitrator). Consequently, before you sign a EULA for a high-tech product or service for your company, you would be wise to have a lawyer read the EULA and explain to you what you are getting into. If you are like most people, when you "purchase" software for your home computer or an app for your smartphone, you click "I agree" without thinking twice about it.

Considerations in Adding High Technology

Business owners are constantly asking themselves if now is the opportunity to add some high technology to their business. The answer is often yes. However, the more important question is, what kind of technology? The timing and type of technology is very important. You don't want to get too far ahead of the curve and purchase technology that is not fully developed for your industry or business. If you do prematurely purchase and implement certain technology, the project could backfire and devastate a previously healthy business. Likewise, you do not want to purchase technology that is either already or soon to be outdated. Therefore, tread carefully in the world of technology and don't believe everything that you are told by some slick salesman trying to sell you the next and best "Quick Books" or "automated" piece of equipment. Do your own research and hire a technology consultant, if necessary. Technology can be your best friend and the best thing in

Technology Timeline

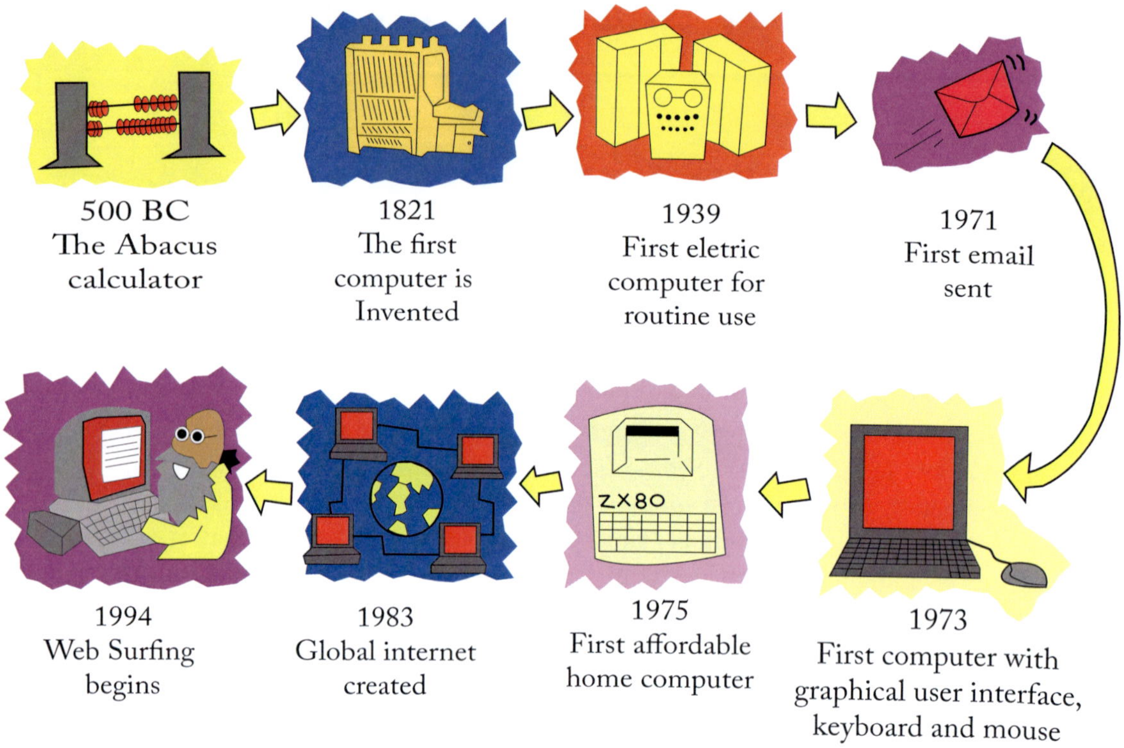

the world but only if it works well. If the technology is flawed, it can be your worst enemy and worst nightmare. It's a "Goldilocks" situation—you don't want technology that's "too cold" (i.e., outdated), and you don't want technology that's "too hot" (i.e., on the bleeding edge of innovation). You want technology that's "just right" for your firm.

So, how do you avoid mistakes in the growing world of everything technology? Define your need for the technology and how you would use it—what exactly do you want it to do for you, and what does it not need to do? Educate yourself, require the producer or vendor to show you how the technology will work best for you, or hire an expert. Make certain that you are not purchasing soon to be outdated technology. "Generally speaking, keeping an eye on the tech press is enough to catch hints for what to expect in the next few months, so get to know the product cycle for whatever it is you're buying, and see what rumors are out there for the next refresh. It's not an exact science but you should at least be able to avoid buying your gadgets at the worst possible time." Make sure your purchased technology will be compatible and will integrate with your other systems. "From something as simple as a phone case to something as sophisticated as a smart TV, you have to make at least a cursory check that your new gear is going to work with all your old gear, otherwise you're setting yourself up for one of the most frustrating cases of buyer's remorse that exists."[1]

Remember, when it looks too good to be true, it probably is. Don't be cheap. "There's a point of false economy you reach when the money you're saving is canceled out by having to upgrade your gear sooner. Sometimes, it's worth paying that little bit extra up front if it means your hardware's going to last longer"[1] and provide a frustration-free experience. Shop around, compare products, compare prices, and know typical pricing and leasing, government grant and tax options. "Taking time to compare prices and tax benefits may mean you miss out on the occasional stellar bargain due to your hesitance, but over the long run you're going to be saving a lot more money if you're careful in your comparisons."[1]

Whether looking at the consumer, small business, or enterprise spaces, usually a mid-range product in a company's product line offers the best value for the dollar. The cheaper product may be a decent budget pick, yet will most likely leave much to be desired with respect to reliability and features, and often will carry a shorter lifespan. The costly version of the product may offer the reliability and features required, but often will contain features paid for that will go unneeded and ultimately unused. As an exercise for the reader, try to think about instances where budget technology was purchased and implemented just to find out shortly thereafter that it is inadequate thereby requiring the project to be performed again, unfortunately costing you time and money. Additionally, there are numerous examples of consumers and businesses being oversold on expensive hardware and software with computing power far exceeding that specific application.

It cannot be emphasized enough the importance of performing your own cursory research before purchasing any technology. It is also important to realize that you may not be an expert in the field, and you should defer to a consultant to make sure the project is done right the first time to provide you a frustration-free experience. To do your own research, there are many great online resources that provide expert reviews. Some examples include: Linus Tech Tips, PCMag, CNET, Tom's Hardware, and iJustine.

Do not impulse buy. "To curb those impulsive behaviors, consider your organization's current needs, workplace culture, and long-term goals—then look for technologies that facilitate those needs." Scrutinize and question everything. "Business owners who lack skepticism need to conduct a feasibility assessment—examining the needs of their business and their employees—before they start looking at tech options." You have to spend money to ultimately save and make money. While the desire to save money is a laudable goal, savvy business owners know that saving money sometimes requires spending money."[2]

Evaluate long term contracts. "Kevin Tash, president and CEO of Tack Media, advises small-business owners against signing long-term contracts. Instead, you should partner with technology vendors that offer flexible subscription-based services. These services tend to adapt to your company's changing needs, allowing it to scale and grow."[2] Examples of subscription-based services would be Google's Application Suite, Microsoft's Office 365, Adobe's Creative Suite, or Amazon Web Services. Subscription-based services tend to provide up to date features and when managed by reputable companies such the ones listed above, generally contain the latest security protocols, 24/7 customer service, flexible pricing (such as, per-user), and a quick product learning curve with efficient workflow tools. Often, people neglect the Information Technology (IT) overhead necessary to actively maintain security, product updates, and employee software training.

The above advice comes with a caveat, like many of the other sentiments shared in this technology section. You must always be cognizant of the limitations of the technology being implemented. Cloud services may be cost effective, offer many features, usability, and customer support; however they would not be suitable for solutions disconnected from the internet nor sectors that handle highly sensitive data (for example, customers' credit card information). No matter the data storage location or security protocols, no data on any server is impervious to attack; cloud solutions are no exception and the flexibility to control your own security protocols on an internal server may be necessary. Ultimately, have a plan and be ready to modify the plan as you learn more or as your business grows.

"Business owners afraid of making the wrong choice should take three steps to come to a decision: First, establish your business needs. Second, review and rank the available technologies. Third, build a proof of concept."[2] Communicate with and educate your staff. "You must communicate about the new technology before, during, and after implementation and offer training and educational resources to help get your team on board."[2] Forecast and measure technology success or failure. "Data, not feelings, should drive your analysis of success. Small business owners should apply logic and analysis throughout their technology implementation.

Proper procurement planning, tax planning, and purchasing standards are essential. In order to make the best purchases you must:[3]

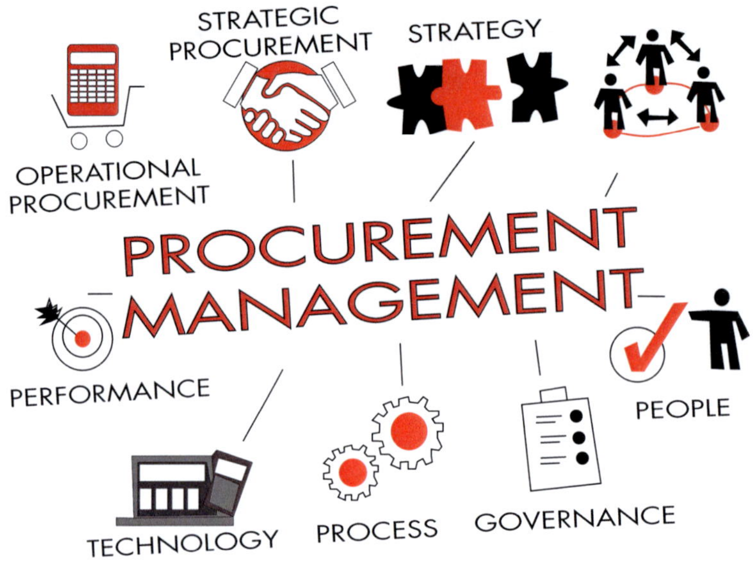

- Negotiate
- Pay attention and communicate with suppliers
- Stay within budget
- Shop around and don't rush purchases
- Involve all decision makers and relevant department heads
- Be flexible
- Establish and follow policy
- Make vendors aware of your policies
- Embrace technology and use it effectively

The time to add technology is for a specific purpose, productivity, cost savings, and growth. Never overbuy on any hardware or software; *function-specific* is what your business should always look for.

> "The more important question is about what they are using the technology for. Instead of using technology to reach the right customer at the right time to convince them to buy a product or service, we're seeing leading companies with the bigger objective of embedding the company, product, or service into their customers' lives. It's less about using technology to sell a product and more about using a suite of technologies that enables a company to partner with consumers on a daily basis to help them achieve their personal goals. That could be about saving for college or feeding a family on a budget."[4]

Finally, it would behoove you to do due diligence on the company that you are buying high technology from. If it is a publicly traded company, there is a great deal of public information about them and their products. If it is a private company, you will have to dig. Standard questions to get answered include: How long have they been in business? How big are they? What is their customer list? Can you get permission to talk with a couple of their customers? What are people saying about the company and the technology on message boards? What are customers saying about the product or service you are considering?

Calculating the Financial Returns

From a business profit and loss standpoint, try to determine the return on investment from the proposed technology addition. How long will it take to implement this technology and what is the learning curve? You only want to purchase new technology if it will take a shorter amount of time to accomplish the task with technology. This time savings must be weighed against the time to develop the technology if creating it from scratch, such as a software tool. A tool will only be beneficial when used frequently, when computation time is far less than human time invested, when the tool can be used by other members of the company in the future, and when the tool is easily modified by a future software developer (not the original creator). A frequent oversight is choice of programming language. In general, the closer the language is to English, the easier it is for a later software programmer to decipher the original code. The trade-off concerns the computation performance – the closer to computer language, the faster the computations and the less storage needed. Therefore, the programming language selection should be determined on a case-by-case basis. Otherwise, you will be putting your business into a negative return on investment without rewarding the business. You never want to see ineffective technology wasting the time of your staff. That wasted time could be used to produce profit. Always strive for an organization that is using technology effectively, with the results being greater than or equal to the resources invested. That's what it means to have a positive Return on Investment (ROI).

> "Return on investment, better known as ROI, is a key performance indicator (KPI) that's often used by businesses to determine profitability of an expenditure. It's exceptionally useful for measuring success over time and taking the guesswork out of making future business decisions...Understanding the importance of ROI is crucial for any business to succeed."[5]

Use ROI analysis to evaluate your already existing technology to drive future technology cost and benefit decision making. Try to assess whether "...expenditures made in proportion to the way technology benefits each of those functional areas. Are you wasting resources on technology that isn't doing much for you? Is your technology budget simply keeping the lights on, or is it fueling your mission?"[6] Return on investment can take into consideration: net present value, internal rate of return, cash flow, payback period, net gain, tax consequences, available grants, and cost. A simple return on investment formula is:

$$\text{ROI} = \frac{\text{Net Gain}}{\text{Cost}} \tag{1}$$

$$\text{ROI} = \frac{\text{(Gain from Investment - Cost Investment)}}{\text{Cost of Investment}} \tag{2}$$

For example, if the business "spends" $10,000 onapieceoftechnologyanditearns 3000$ per year, its ROI over a 5-year period is:

$$\text{ROI} = \frac{((\$3000 \times 5\text{Years}) - \$10,000)}{\$10,000} = .5 \Rightarrow 50\% \tag{3}$$

In order to turn the ROI fraction into percentage, multiply by 100. An ROI of .5, multiplied by 100, equals a 50% ROI. Therefore, there is a 50% return on investment after 5 years. This is a good benchmark to achieve, being able to pay off your investment in 5 years or less. After five years or greater, everything that is earned is profit and the technology can be fully depreciated, or if leased written off as a business tax deduction or tax credit. Government grants may also be available. This is an oversimplified example for ease of concept understanding purposes. Other cost variables to consider and include in the cost are:

- Training and Support
- Disposal or recycling of old technology
- Disruption and frustration
- Staff Time
- Opportunity cost
- Upgrades and maintenance

Opportunity cost is an interesting variable. When making a business purchase, it should be analyzed if those same funds could be better spent on alternatives to make more profit and achieve more growth. If the answer is yes, that you can achieve more growth without the new technology; however, if you choose to implement that technology anyway, you must factor in the opportunity you lost to make more money—a monetary value known as opportunity cost. All decisions have a positive and negative value. Try to use all those values to help make each and every business decision in determining the best "positive" opportunity for profits and growth.

Simply put, you want to forecast what your new technology costs and what your return on investments will be, in order to make sound purchase or non-purchase decisions. While making your technology decisions, explore and attempt to innovate new or increased revenue streams, a broader reach of products and services, and other growth avenues while taking advantage of every government tax and grant opportunity.

When investing in new technology, equipment, or machinery, consult with your accountant, tax lawyer, business consultant, and economic development offices. There are many government incentives that could be available to help subsidize or offset its cost. One tremendous government incentive is "Section 179" of the U.S. IRS Tax Code.[7] Section 179 allows a business to deduct the eligible "total equipment purchased" cost, whether purchased outright or leased in the same calendar year as the transaction. In 2018, Section 179 allowed "...up to one million dollars in eligible equipment to be deducted, and the 'total equipment purchased' by a business cannot exceed $2.5 million. Once the equipment purchased exceeds that number, the deduction reduces on a dollar for dollar basis. Also, businesses with a net loss in a given tax year qualify to carry-forward the Bonus Depreciation to a future year. When applying these provisions, Section 179 is generally taken first, followed by Bonus Depreciation – unless the business has no taxable profit in the given tax year."[8] This dollar amount and deduction can change from year to year. Therefore, you must check with your tax professional. Interestingly, don't be surprised if "the taxes you save with the deduction will almost always exceed your cash outlay for the year when you combine (i) a properly structured Equipment Lease or Equipment Finance Agreement with (ii) a full Section 179 deduction."[8] Again, check with and strategize these tax savings with your tax advisor.

In addition to tax deductions, your business might also qualify for the general business tax credit or government grant. Tax credits directly reduce your tax liability dollar for dollar and are more valuable than a tax deduction, which only help to reduce your tax liability by lowering your tax bracket.

> "The general business tax credit is a non-refundable credit that directly reduces the tax bill. It can only reduce a taxpayer's liability to zero; any amount that remains from the credit is automatically forfeited by the taxpayer. In addition, it can only be claimed after all other available non-refundable credits have been used, except for the Alternative Minimum Tax (AMT) credit. General business tax credit for the year consists of an entity's carryforward of business credits from prior years plus the total of its current year business credits. Unused credit must first be carried back one year, then carried forward for up to 20 years. With regards to the both the carryforward as well as the carryback provisions, the first-in first-out (FIFO) method is applied, which results in older credits being applied first, thereby, reducing the chance of credit expiration moving forward."[9]

Some examples of general business tax credits are: "Investment and Research Credit (Form 3468), Work Opportunity Credit (Form 5884), Low-Income Housing Credit (Form 8586), Disabled Access Credit (Form 8826), Energy Efficient Home Credit (Form 8908), Credit for Employer-Provided Childcare Facilities and Services (Form 8882), Credit for Small Employer Pension Plan Startup Costs (Form 8881), Credit for Employer Social Security and Medicare Taxes Paid on Certain Employee Tips (Form 8846), Qualified plug-in electric drive motor vehicle credit (Form 8936)."[9]

Because tax credit opportunities can change from year to year, always check with your tax planner in advance of any purchases or commitments. Government grants are low interest long term government loans for materials, equipment, machinery, real estate, projects, etc., that are forgiven and free when certain criteria are met; such as increased number of employees or meeting certain tax dollar generation amounts that help offset the government grant. These tax credits and grants are well worth looking into for the opportunity of increased free money, profit, and growth while preserving business capital. On a federal level, refer to the Federal Economic Development Administration (EDA) website[10] for more details. Every state also has an EDA.

Technology is your friend when wise decisions are made. Always be on the lookout for the next best technology that will increase profits, increase growth, keep you competitive, and outpace your competition.

Major Takeaway

Unless developing a consumer technology from scratch, it is generally not a good idea to be the first one on the block to implement new or newly updated software or technology. Let others go first, suffer with its bugs and flaws, and let them do all of the complaining and reporting. Thereafter, when the bugs and flaws are removed and patches are applied to the software by the software company, or a newly released version is available, then implement or do the installation. Avoid technology headaches, when possible.

Microsoft Windows 8 is the perfect example of not wanting to get ahead of technology and risking software malfunction.

> "Deplored by many for its removal of Windows' iconic "Start" button, Windows 8 in 2012 was the biggest rethink of Microsoft's too-big-to-fail computing linchpin

> since Redmond first slapped a "Start" button in Windows 95's lower left-hand corner. Consumers weren't sure what to make of Microsoft's colorful, tile-driven "Metro" interface, which worked fine on the company's fledgling Surface tablets, but felt convoluted on laptops and desktops (which went on to account for virtually all of Windows 8's market share). This merging was arguably brilliant and too far ahead of its time."[11]

Having a single operating system that spans desktops, laptops, tablets, and smartphones sounds like a great idea. Having a single user interface that spans desktops, laptops, tablets, and smartphones sounds like a terrible idea. Microsoft did it anyway with Windows 8, but fixed the problem in Windows 10.[12]

Another great example for walking, not running, and "easing" into technology advances is the digital camera and digital technology. For years, the argument was digital or film. Until about a decade of better digital technology, the answer was film. Then the science of digital camera sensors improved decreasing *pixilation*. The digital pictures are now clearer than film and digitally transferable. The rest is digital history as nobody uses film anymore.

Kodak Digital Camera System, 1991: Built around the body of a Nikon F3, the Digital Camera System was the first to put the "D" in front of "SLR." Kodak engineers replaced the back of the Nikon shooter with a digital panel that contained a 1.3-megapixel color or monochrome image sensor in a 1024 x 1280 pixel array. Pictures were piped from the camera directly to an attached hard drive with a preview screen. Though modern cameras are substantially more compact and self-contained, at the core, they all function much like the original Kodak system.[13] However, film icon, Kodak, did not put enough R&D into future generation digital products, lost too much market share to its competitors, and went out of business.

Therefore, if you invest in new technology too soon: it will be more expensive, not be as good as later generation technology development, or you may find that the company that you purchased from is out of business. The best advice is to watch the technology evolve and purchase the technology that you need when prices come down, only purchase from a strong and reliable company, and only purchase after the technology has been better perfected to suit all your requirements for a reasonable amount of time. Again, you do not want to purchase and invest in technology that will be outdated or fail in a short period of time.

References

1. David Nield. *5 Stupid Mistakes to Avoid When Buying New Tech*. Jan. 2018. URL: https://gizmodo.com/5-stupid-mistakes-to-avoid-when-buying-new-tech-1822161165 (cited on page 126).

2. Alec Sears. *7 Mistakes to Avoid When Buying New Technology for Your Business*. May 2018. URL: http://www.liveplan.com/blog/2018/05/7-mistakes-to-avoid-when-buying-new-technology-for-your-business/ (cited on page 127).

3. *10 Most Costly Procurement Mistakes and How to Avoid Them*. Aug. 2017. URL: http://www.nextprocess.com/procurement-solutions/common-procurement-mistakes-and-how-to-avoid-them/ (cited on page 127).

4. Steve Olenski. *The 5 Technology Trends That May Disrupt Business Over The Next 3 Years*. Mar. 2018. URL: http://www.forbes.com/sites/steveolenski/2018/03/12/the-5-technology-trends-that-may-disrupt-business-over-the-next-3-years/ (cited on page 128).
5. Erica Hawkins. *The Importance of ROI | Call Tracking and Analytics*. Aug. 2018. URL: http://www.callrail.com/blog/importance-of-roi-why-it-matters-for-all-businesses/ (cited on page 129).
6. Karen Graham. *Measuring Return on Investment for Technology*. June 2015. URL: http://www.idealware.org/measuring-return-investment-technology/ (cited on page 129).
7. U.S. Code 26 §179. Election to expense certain depreciable business assets (cited on page 130).
8. *Section 179 Information for Businesses*. URL: https://www.section179.org/ (cited on page 130).
9. Julia Kagan. *General Business Tax Credit*. May 2018. URL: https://www.investopedia.com/terms/g/general-business-tax-credit.asp (cited on page 131).
10. *Funding Opportunities*. URL: http://www.eda.gov/funding-opportunities/ (cited on page 131).
11. Lisa Eadicicco et al. *TIME's 20 Most Successful Technology Failures of All Time*. Apr. 2017. URL: http://time.com/4704250/most-successful-technology-tech-failures-gadgets-flops-bombs-fails/ (cited on page 132).
12. Zach Epstein. *5 awful Windows 8 problems that are fixed in Windows 10*. July 2015. URL: https://bgr.com/2015/07/29/windows-10-features-fixed-problems-windows-8/ (cited on page 132).
13. John Henshall. *Kodak Digital Cameras*. May 1993. URL: http://www.epi-centre.com/reports/9306cs.html (cited on page 132).

XVI

Opportunity To Update/Add Website And Social Media

The Rationale, in Brief

Imagine a store in which there is a business. But the building the store is in does not have the name of the business on it. Nor is there any information about where the building is located. There is no information about what the business does (does it make toys, does it handle international legal transactions, or does it do something else?completely unclear). No phone number is provided. No indication of the hours it is open is given. Just how successful do you think this business is going to be?

If your firm does not have a website and a social media presence, your firm is like the above business. For the millions (and rapidly growing!) who only shop online, your firm is invisible; effectively, your firm does not exist. Especially for the younger, technologically hip generation, the internet and social media are where they spend most of their personal and professional lives. You simply must exist in cyberspace. You may think it is all silly, but your customers do not, especially the younger customers who will evolve to be the only customers out there.

Not only do you need a website and a social media presence, yours must be compelling – fast to load, easiest to do business with, extremely clear and transparent, identical whether on cell phone, laptop, tablet, or desktop machine, and significantly better than those of your competitors. Finally, your firm will need to constantly tweak your website and social media presence. Being static and unchanging is boring and fails to take advantage of ever changing technology and customers? preferences and tastes.

Overview

Websites, *blogs*, *e-newsletters*, and *social media* are the new norm. Every business must have a website URL (URL stands for Uniform Resource Locators, or the web address) and a social media identity to thrive and grow. The sooner, the better, is always advisable. The start-up does not even need to start in order to exist in cyberspace. Register your space on the internet super highway before someone else occupies it. Consumers are on the go and always choosing their next steps on their work computers, smartphones, or other mobile devices. Do not miss the opportunity!

To develop your website and social media presence, have in mind a business and marketing plan. What are you selling? This plan will help dictate the name of your company, and the name of the website and social media pages. Sometimes, they can be one and the same. Other times, they cannot. For example, you might have chosen a great name for your business, but it might not be available as a URL on the internet for your website or social media. The name might have already been taken by someone else. Now what? Either use a different name than your company name for your website and social media, regroup, and choose an available internet name first, then name the company thereafter.

Hosting and e-commerce platforms are also important. Technology changes rapidly; do your homework. It will be important to choose the hosting and e-commerce platform that will work well for your business and its customers. Plan on updating. However, now that you already own your website URL and have a business name, you should now claim your social media sites. Go ahead and get started creating social media pages to post on sites such as Facebook and LinkedIn, since those are platforms that already exist. You can be completing your social media presence while you are planning your website. Get those social media sites done first since they only take about a day each to complete without comprehensive technical expertise. This way you have some presence while you are building the website that can take a week to a month to build. Take a multifaceted, multi-tasked approach to creating and completing your on-line presence.

Maintaining Your Website

Once your website is built, you can?t forget about it. Websites will require constant updates and Search Engine Optimization (SEO) analysis for success. (SEO refers to the process of attempting to get your website listed as early as possible when a search engine such as Google or Bing is used to search for your type of business.) ?Avoid bit decay; the site needs maintenance. Technology is ever changing and hopefully your business is keeping up. You need a plan to update, maintain, and improve your website on a monthly, if not weekly basis. Ask yourself, How is my target audience changing, and how can I quickly adapt to their needs?[1] This includes changes in website content and format. Page alternations, additions, and removal are necessary in keeping your website up to date.

When updating a website, your URL should be maintained as best as possible since other websites may have linked to a specific page on your website. Too often, we encounter broken URLs. These URLs and potential links to your page should be maintained since they drive people to your site and consequently improve SEO.

In the process of maintaining a website, you may conclude that your website may need to be completely redesigned to accommodate changing user interfaces, content, and format. Building a website from scratch is relatively difficult to accomplish and costly to maintain.

Depending upon the type of content you would like to deliver, a custom website may be necessary. In most cases though, a custom site is not necessary and an already developed platform such as WordPress, Drupal, or Joomla may fit the bill nicely while saving money in the long run by saving you from costly custom website development. An additional feature of these free, off-the-shelf content management systems is a well-refined graphical user interface backend where somebody with limited web design knowledge can quickly and efficiently update website content with predefined formats. This mitigates the need for a costly web developer to make changes each time you or your staff would like to update the website.

We have come a long way since the first baby steps of the World Wide Web. Back in January of 1996 there were 100,000 websites, and if we go back to mid-1993 there were only a total of 130 websites.[2] For good business reason, the growth of the internet is staggering. More than 140,000 websites are launched every day. In 1991 the first website came on-line.[3] Ten years later, in 2001, there were 40 million websites. According to 2008 numbers, there were 162 million websites on the internet. Thereafter, in 2011 there were 644 million websites, a 1500% increase.[4] Today, in 2018, there are over 1.8 billion websites, a 300% increase in 7 years.[5]

Even with these enormous amounts of websites, it is surprising to learn that as of 2018, 60% of

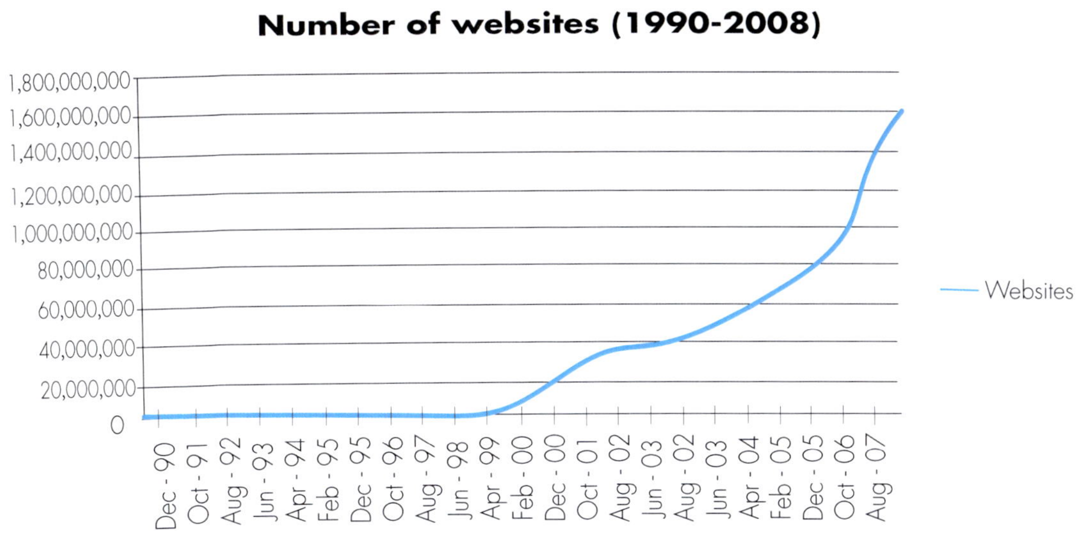

Number of websites between 1990 and 2008.[2]

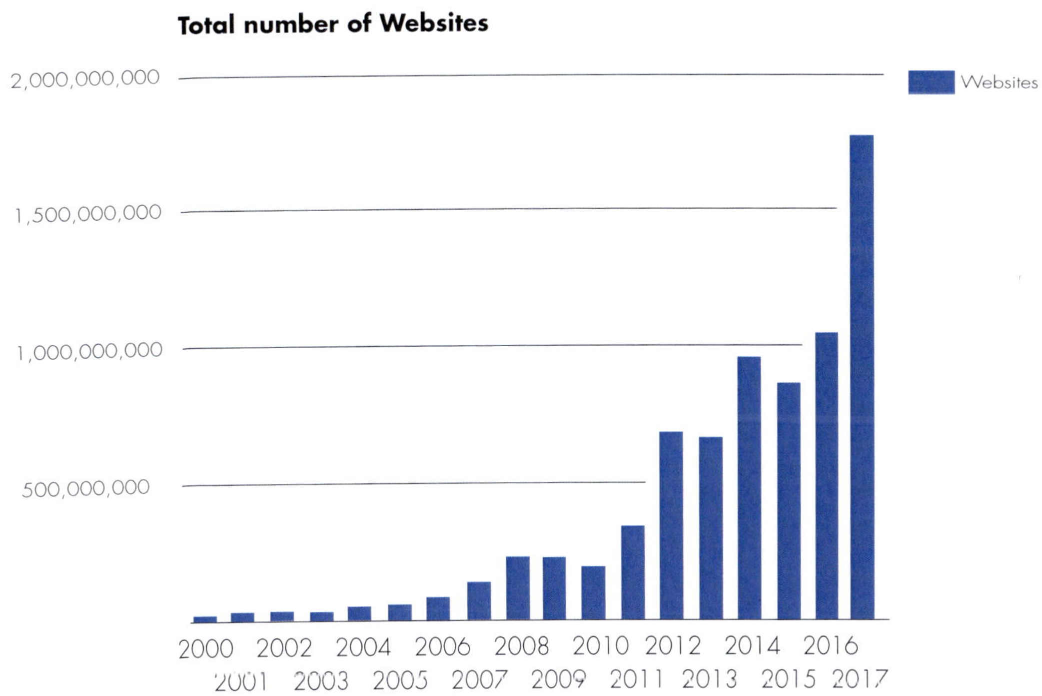

Number of websites between 2000 and 2017.[5]

small business is still operating without a website. Of those 60% that do not have websites, 12% do have Facebook pages. Of the 40% of surveyed businesses that do have websites, 83% said their online platforms gave them a competitive advantage over businesses without websites.[6]

Importance of a Digital Presence

Amazingly, many small businesses are still not connected to the internet by website or social media. So, what does this mean? It means that businesses are still missing the opportunity to update or add a website and social media, i.e., important advertising opportunities. Therefore, by starting a website, updating this website, and maintaining a website and social media regularly, you will still gain a competitive advantage over those businesses without websites. Also, by adding or updating websites and social media, a business can stay competitive with those businesses that already have websites. This website and social media information demonstrate the need for a business website and social media platform to compete with those who have one, and out compete those who do not. "...According to Clutch's third annual Small Business Survey, small businesses continuously struggle to create and maintain a web presence."[6]

The big question is why? Here are some reasons for the lack of website or social media presence. Using these reasons as examples, we will provide solutions so that you don't lose your "opportunity" to capture more business and better brand awareness. "It is more important than ever to have a responsive [desktop and mobile-friendly], well designed website for your small business...Whether you are just starting out, think the web isn't related to your industry, or don't think you have the time and money, launching a website needs to be a top priority."[7]

Wonder why "Low-revenue small businesses (those earning less than $1 million a year) are about 30% less likely to have a website than higher-revenue companies."[7] Simple, maybe it's because they don't have a website. It's the dog chasing its tail syndrome. I don't make enough money to start a website. If I only had a website, I can make more money. It's a fact, those businesses with websites will gross higher revenues. Why do businesses with websites have higher grosses?

Businesses with websites possess many advantages over those that do not have websites:

- Increased marketing and sales opportunities
- Better brand awareness
- Cost effectiveness
- Lead generation
- Business analytics
- Sales tracking
- Mobile phone capability

Then, what is the business reason or excuse for not having a website? Is It because:

- They are not "tech savvy"?
- A website appears to certain business owners as overwhelming?
- Think it will be too expensive and not cost effective?
- Lack understanding of business importance?

- Believe they lack financial resources?
- Claim a website is not relevant?
- Are not aware of the revenue loss?

You will get some curmudgeons out there that say, "I don't need a stinking website." They'll call me up and say, "I really don't think my industry is on the Internet, but I wanted to get your opinion." And so, I say "OK, I want you to Google this." And then they go, "Oh my god, everybody's on the Internet. My competitors are there. I'm behind the times" -Alan Dale, Los Angeles Web Design.[7]

Ironically, businesses have a hard time understanding lost business that they don't have. Are there viable substitutes to a website? Yes and no. "Of the small businesses without a website, 31% instead use social media profiles to cultivate a web presence."[7] As the saying goes, "something is better than nothing." If the business does not have a website, at least it has some presence on social media. Ultimately, the goal is to get your marketing working seamlessly on all cylinders that will interact for maximum brand awareness and sales as soon as possible. It is ideal to have a website, blog, newsletter, and social media operating in tandem together with links to one another.

Bottom line, there are more than one-half the earth's population of 4 billion potential customers on the internet each and every day.[8] It is in the best interest of the business to expose your business, products, and services to all those consumers and potential customers.

A Primer on Website Design

While it is optimal to use an experienced professional to design your website, it is not uncommon to do it yourself. If the latter, begin by looking at some websites and finding a few that your really admire. Often, those will be from well-known, large, successful firms such as Apple or Ford. Ask yourself what you like about those sites—often, people will mention that they look "clean" with no distractions, they are clear, text is not jarring (e.g., no strange colors or odd fonts), it is easy to find what you are looking for, it is easy to figure out how to contact them, and they appear to be complete.

Then, look at some sites from small, local companies (e.g., George's Garage or Fred's Flowers). Often, there will be something about those sites that is irritating or that suggests an amateur put the site together (for example, the photos are fuzzy, it is unclear if the prices listed are still in effect today, or there is an overwhelming amount of text to read).

Then make a list of what your site should look like, and what it should not look like. Typically, in a lower corner, indicate when it was last updated and by whom. If you are not comfortable using HTML, you will want to use a professional to create the site, but you can instruct the professional as to what you definitely want on your site and what you definitely don't want your site to resemble. Typically, a good website helps visitors understand: where is your firm, what hours is it open, how do they reach you by email, fax and phone, what you do you sell, what are current prices, do you offer any guarantees or warranties, who are the leaders of your team and what are their backgrounds, anticipate frequently asked questions (FAQx) and provide answers, why should people do business with you, provide a few testimonials from satisfied customers, provide links to those social media sites your firm is listed on, and help people navigate around your website. There should be helpful photos, and if a complicated process needs to be explained, a short video or two is in order (YouTube is a godsend).

A professional may suggest other features that your unique business should include (or exclude)

Share of individuals using the internet, 2015

Share of individuals using the internet, measured as the percentage of the population. Internet users are individuals who have used the Internet (from any location) in the last 3 months. The Internet can be used via a computer, mobile phone, personal digital, assistant game machine, digital TV, etc.

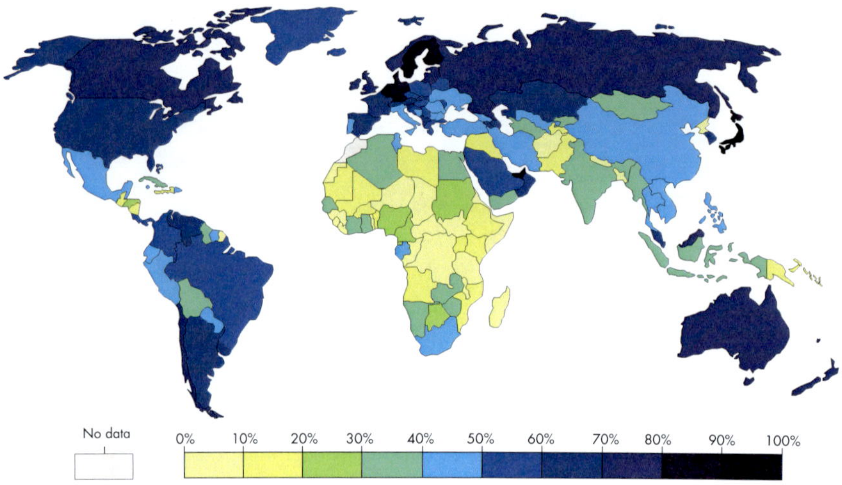

Source: World Bank

Mobile cellular subscriptions (per100 people) - 2015

Mobile phone subscriptions. Measured as the number per100 people

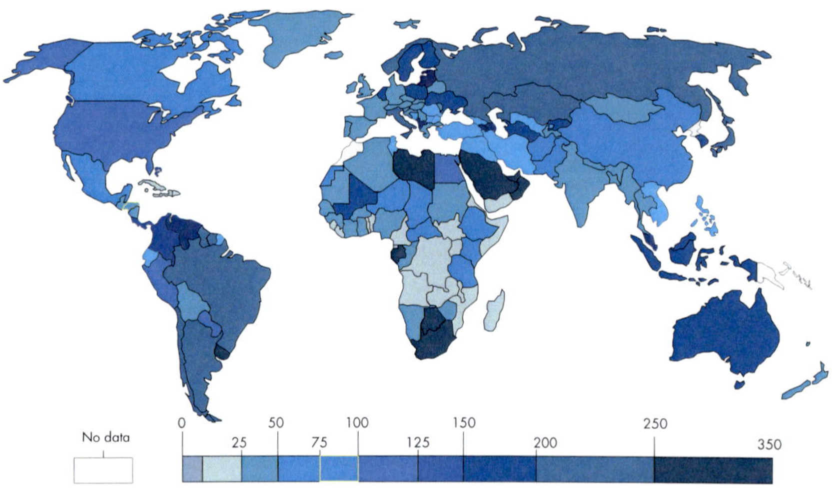

Source: World Bank

World map of internet access and map of mobile phone subscriptions.[9]

for your website. The professional will ensure that your site loads quickly, and that it looks attractive on a number of different browsers such as Google Chrome, Mozilla Firefox, Opera, Microsoft Edge, and others. Professionals will ensure that relevant keywords are put in your site's metadata, along with other information used by search engines.

Once your website is "up," ask a few friends and key employees to look at it and provide their feedback. Once the design is "final," turn it live (i.e., release it on the internet), but be prepared to revise and edit it roughly every quarter, once you start hearing from customers as to what they like, what they dislike, and what they wish was on your website.

Major Takeaway

Do your website right the first time! Here is an example of the very popular "Game of Thrones" author first generation website, followed by his next attempt. Lesson learned, get it right the first time to best brand your stellar reputation and save money.

George R.R. Martin's Initial Website (www.georgerrmartin.com)

George R.R. Martin's Improved Website (www.georgerrmartin.com)

Case Study

Our consulting firm was hired to assist with a business start-up. Unfortunately, before we were hired, the owners did not have a business plan. They had named and registered the business with the state, then registered a low-cost and nondescript domain name not realizing that the domain name was too long. In addition, the business and website names did not describe the business. During the consultation period, we came up with a shortened website name that properly described the business, and added a slogan to the business name that also properly described the business. As we explained in the chapter, if the owners had a business plan that addressed the business name and website together; there is a good likelihood the client might have done their proper research and named the business and website correctly.

References

1. Adam Hayes. *Succeed Online*. URL: http://www.ahfx.net/weblog/120 (cited on page 138).
2. *How we got from 1 to 162 million websites on the internet*. Apr. 2008. URL: https://royal.pingdom.com/how-we-got-from-1-to-162-million-websites-on-the-internet/ (cited on pages 138, 139).
3. *World Wide Web*. URL: http://info.cern.ch/hypertext/WWW/TheProject.html (cited on page 138).
4. Julie Bort. *How Many Web Sites Are There?* Mar. 2012. URL: http://www.businessinsider.com/how-many-web-sites-are-are-there-2012-3 (cited on page 138).
5. *How Many Websites Are There Around the World?* Feb. 2019. URL: https://www.millforbusiness.com/how-many-websites-are-there/ (cited on pages 138, 139).
6. Tess Townsend. *Many Small Businesses Have Little to No Online Presence*. Sept. 2015. URL: http://www.inc.com/tess-townsend/small-business-survey-godaddy-websites.html (cited on page 140).
7. Amelia Peacock. *Small business websites in 2017: Survey*. Mar. 2017. URL: https://clutch.co/web-designers/resources/small-business-2017-website-survey (cited on pages 140, 141).
8. Miniwatts Marketing Group. *Internet World Stats: Usage and Population Statistics*. June 2018. URL: https://www.internetworldstats.com/stats.htm (cited on page 141).
9. Julia Murphy and Max Roser. "Internet". In: *Our World in Data* (2019). https://ourworldindata.org/intern (cited on page 142).

VII Is Now The Opportunity To Invest In R&D?

Overview of R&D

The term **research** is used in every scientific and industrial field, however its implications and implementation may vary greatly between fields. Here, we break down what the word research means – in broad terms, its impact on business and profitability, impact on society, and how to successfully implement research into your business plan. Broadly, research encompasses the scientific method comprising of the systematic gathering of information and understanding of the information gathered in the advancement of knowledge. This is, of course, is only the research aspect of research and development with the other aspect being *development*.

In order to bring a technology discovered by research to market, refinements of the technology must be made with respect to form and function. Using the engineering design process as a guide, the first phase in the process is research, then followed by the development phases: design requirements, feasibility, conceptualization, preliminary design, detailed design, design of manufacturability, and production planning.

According to the Accrediting Board for Engineering and Technology, Inc (ABET), "it is a decision making process (often iterative) in which the basic sciences, mathematics, and engineering sciences are applied to convert resources optimally to meet a stated objective. Among the fundamental elements of the design process are the establishment of objectives and criteria, synthesis, analysis, construction, testing and evaluation."[1]

> "Research and experimental development (R&D) comprise creative and systematic work undertaken in order to increase the stock of knowledge—including knowledge of humankind, culture and society—and to devise new applications of available knowledge. A set of common features identifies R&D activities, even if these are carried out by different performers. R&D activities may be aimed at achieving either specific or general objectives. R&D is always aimed at new findings, based on original concepts (and their interpretation) or hypotheses. It is largely uncertain about its final outcome (or at least about the quantity of time and resources needed to achieve it), it is planned for and budgeted (even when carried out by individuals), and it is aimed at producing results that could be either freely transferred or traded in a marketplace. For an activity to be an R&D activity, it must satisfy five core criteria.
>
> The activity must be:
>
> - novel
> - creative
> - uncertain
> - systematic
> - transferable and/or reproducible."[2]

More specifically, business research and development (R&D) "comprise [of] creative and systematic work undertaken in order to increase the stock of knowledge and to devise new applications of available knowledge. This includes

1. Activities aimed at acquiring new knowledge or understanding without specific immediate commercial applications or uses (basic research)

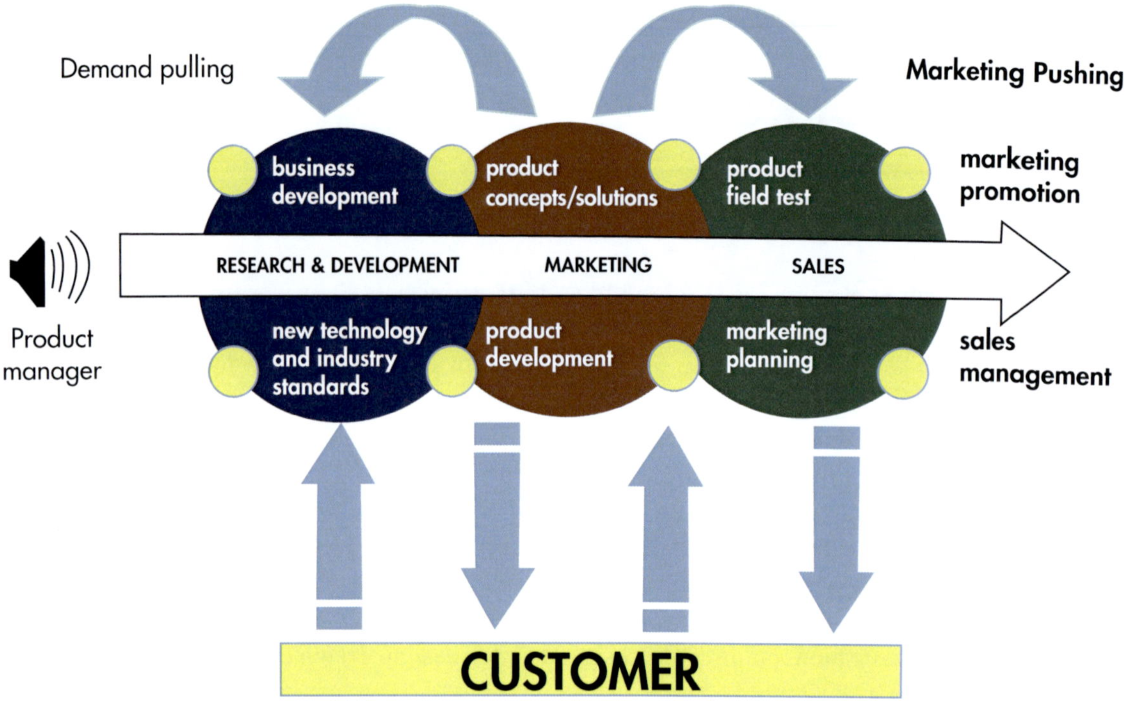

2. Activities aimed at solving a specific problem or meeting a specific commercial objective (applied research)
3. Systematic work, drawing on research and practical experience and resulting in additional knowledge, which is directed to producing new products or processes or to improving existing products or processes (development).

R&D includes both direct costs such as salaries of researchers as well as administrative and overhead costs clearly associated with the company's R&D."[2]

Phases of R&D

Now that we have established what R&D is,

- When does a business begin its R&D?
- What will the R&D be?
- How will it be applied to the business?

These are very important questions that need to be answered before embarking on R&D projects in business. That's right, you need a plan.

Like any other business topic, R&D should be a section of your business plan. If you did not originally include R&D, or the R&D section was written a while ago and is now outdated, it is time to revise the business plan with the:

- types of R&D required for success.
- description of your current R&D budget.
- staff and outside contract capacity and resources.
- R&D agenda with timeline.

- R&D expenditure timeline.
- R&D short and long-term goals.

"Research and development, known as R&D, refers to that part of your business plan that is your ability to gain knowledge in order to design, develop, and enhance your product, services, technologies, or processes. If your company is a high-tech firm, R&D is number one on the list of capabilities crucial to your long-term success."[3]

Every business requires some form of R&D. "For example, a business that liquidates households for people who can't do so on their own hardly seems in need of R&D capability. But, think again. The Internet now plays a starring role in the sale of antiques and collectibles — whether through online auctions or through specialized auction and antique sales sites. And even if the business owners never go near an online sale, almost certainly they'll use online resources to find out what people are paying for items like the ones they're selling.

For other businesses, R&D is the key to enhancing business skills, enlarging product and service portfolios, and staying on top of customer, industry, and competitive research. Ways to improve your R&D skills include: Attending trade shows with research-related sessions, Taking industry-specific courses, in person or online, Participating in social media networks with people in your field who share findings, ideas, and advice, Subscribing to mailings from innovators in your industry, Completing certification programs, Updating computer skills, keeping up-to-date through trade journals and sites, joining an industry group, broadening your awareness of industry, market area, consumer, and industry issues and opportunities"[3]

End Goals of R&D

If you're a technology or pharmaceutical company, R&D is a lifeline to the business. The new software or medications developed are put in commerce and ultimately sold to consumers. Pharmaceuticals are also patented to protect the company from competition for twenty years in order to recoup their investment and be rewarded for being the first to market with an invention.

When looking at patents and copyrights on technology such as software, it may or may not be patented or copywritten depending on its use and distribution. And, the differentiation is quite interesting. An issued patent can be used to prevent others from utilizing an inventive aspect of a new software program, or from implementing the distinguishing characteristic of a new website. For instance, Apple has patented the 'bounce-back' feature of iOS, in which a list of items stretches beyond the last item and then bounces back when a user comes to the end of the list. Apple has used this patent to prevent its Android competitors from copying this aspect of its user interface. Similarly, Google has numerous patents on its PageRank system, which helped prevent others from copying Google's search algorithm in its early days of competition with Yahoo, Altavista, and Excite.

In contrast, copyright law can only prevent the copying of a particular expression of an idea (see `http://www.BitLaw.com` for their discussion of copyright rights). In connection with computer software, copyright law can be used to prevent the total duplication of a software program, as well as the copying of a portion of software code (both of which are examples of "literal infringement"). In addition, copyright does provide some protection against non-literal infringement, such as the creation of 'cloned' software. However, courts have recently been reluctant to interpret copyright protection of computer software in a broad manner. In addition, the basic tenet of copyright law is that copyright will protect only the expression of an idea, and not the idea itself. Consequently, copyright law will not prevent the creation of a competing program that utilizes the same ideas as an existing program.[4]

"Due to the complex requirements for the grant of patents, the costs for obtaining and enforcing a patent may be costly. Unless you have important financial resources, it may be worth considering whether patenting your software-related innovation is the best way to protect your product. The possibility and feasibility of using other types of intellectual property, such as trademarks, industrial designs and trade secret protection, may also be considered."[5]

On a less scientific or technology note, let's say a business is a corrugated box manufacturer and invents a new box shape, design, and assembly configuration; this is a patent opportunity that should be applied for. However, if a food business develops a new recipe, the recipe should not be patented. Treat it as a trade secret. This is why it is vital to have a business plan that includes R&D – in order to know how inventions will be protected and handled. As demonstrated, "R&D's business value contribution needs to align to an organization's vision, objectives, and strategies with greater transparency. A strategic cross-functional approach that identifies and integrates critical management functions, processes, alliances, tools, and metrics is crucial to developing an R&D organization that cultivates success and delivers expectations."[5]

Making discoveries and inventing cost money. A business must be ready to budget for R&D in order to improve already existing products and functions with an eye on return on investment and profit. Most businesses set aside reasonable amounts of money and resources towards R&D. Some industries must spend a lot more than other industry averages as their reasonable cost of doing business. Computing, electronics, and healthcare companies spend the highest annual percentage of R&D dollars at 23 percent (typically, R&D expenditures are given as a percentage of the firm's revenues). Consumer and telecom companies spend the least R&D annual percentage of revenue at about 2 percent. In order to stay competitive in your business industry, you would not want to spend more than the industry average in order to be competitive; unless the business is disrupting and transforming the industry.[6] Most firms find themselves spending 3%-5% on R&D. Some firms spend half on "R" alone, while other firms find themselves spending most on just "D."

Three types of R&D that companies typically invest in are: basic research, applied research, and development. Basic research might be of interest to a company for knowledge, but not for profit. Applied research focuses on products and processes for commercialization. Development implements the research into the development of prototypes, processes, materials, systems, methods and engineered commercial products. In addition to R&D costs, there are innovation, new product development, design, and product design expenses to bring new or improved products and processes to market.

After deciding to invest in R&D, the business must then make several other decisions on how the R&D will be accomplished. Will the business have its own R&D facility, or will it outsource the R&D? Generally, it is a good idea to outsource the R&D with nondisclosure agreements if the product cannot be patented. The theory behind this decision is that if you will not get a patent that will protect the product and provide a head start into the marketplace, then expend less money by outsourcing the R&D since it can be easily copied by a competitor. Risk is another factor. In order to minimize R&D risk, the business can acquire the technology contingent upon testing and approval before purchase of the product. Cost is also a major factor in the decision to do R&D in-house versus outsourcing. If this product will be in long term use, you are better off insourcing rather than expending long term license and royalty fees, unless the product is able to be purchased outright at less than the cumulative fees. When outsourcing R&D, always be on the lookout for restrictive covenants and regional barriers that could prohibit the use of the product in your areas of potential release and use. Needless to say, assess all the pros and cons when deciding on R&D plans and whether the product will be insourced, outsourced, or purchased.

Once the business has decided to invest in R&D, the business must understand certain basic requirements. In order to create a successful research and development program: constantly evaluate needs, satisfy objectives, have goals and timelines, put together a talented team, and be ready to outsource as needed. There are many advantages to having your own research and development department. Those advantages include but are not limited to:[7]

- tax deductions and credits,
- reduction of costs and increases in profit margin,
- increased investor financing,
- recruiting more highly qualified talent, and
- a valuable patent library.

When evaluating the R&D requirements and its advantages, do a risk/benefit analysis to determine whether an R&D program will be an investment that will be of value and profitable for your business.[8] R&D is a big business – breeding innovation, business growth, and employment. In 2015, United States businesses spent $356 billion on R&D.[9] Federal government grants provided private businesses with $26 billion of grant money. The return on investment can be calculated with, "The most common approach to measuring returns relies on the estimation of a production function which relates investment inputs (most often expenditure on R&D) to a measure of output or productivity."[10] When evaluating "production function methods, the existing literature tends to estimate private rates of return to R&D investments of around 30% (mean) or 20 to 25% (median) and social returns, based on spillover benefits from R&D conducted by one agent to the productivity or output of other agents, are typically 2 to 3 times larger than private returns."[10] Therefore, taking into consideration proper R&D planning, government funding, branding awareness benefits, and 25% cash return on investment; R&D is a good and necessary strategy for every business to grow and survive.

Major Takeaway

The best way to understand and learn the importance of research and development is to look at the history of important inventions. The top 5 inventions as voted by a group of 12 scientists, technology executives, and technology historians are:

1. Printing Press
2. Electricity
3. Penicillin
4. Semiconductor
5. Optical lenses

As you go through the list, see if you agree. Without the printing press, there would have been no early communication for human information and collaboration on all levels. It can be said that the invention of the printing press gave rise to our digital age of information today. Humans crave information. Most of that original information that is on the internet today was first printed on a printing press.

Electricity is a next natural choice, printing presses and other machines before electricity were run manually or by mechanical means, causing the yearning for *automated* tools and equipment.

Penicillin, the first antibiotic and pharmaceutical that makes the list, realizing without health and life, none of these other R&D innovations could occur. Penicillin was accidentally discovered by Alexander Fleming in 1929, and in the spirit of this chapter's lessons regarding research and development, it is worthwhile to mention that while trying to reach an objective, some advancements are discovered by accident and an open mind should be maintained during the research process. Following the research phase, penicillin was developed/refined by researchers at Oxford University to cure soldiers' bacterial infections during World War Two.

This was a major invention to prevent death from pathogenic bacteria and keep our soldiers on the battlefield fighting for our freedoms. It is also important to mention that much research occurs in the public sector, and may even be accidentally and through technology transfer at public institutions, can make their way to the private sector.

Semiconductors expanded the importance of the earlier development of electricity allowing for the development of digital technologies compared to their analog counterpart of yesteryear. Semiconductors, and consequently transistor development, allow for unparalleled computation power and electrical devices that are smaller, more efficient, and more reliable due to improved electricity conductivity methods and materials.

Then there are optical lenses, originally invented for humans to see better after their vision deteriorates. Today, that same optical lens technology of yesterday helped to revolutionize today's scanning machines, compact discs, barcode scanners, vehicle headlight technology, photography, filmmaking, holography, entertainment, and the advancement of other important research fields such as laser/optical physics; resulting in the invention of computer optical drives. The great innovations in optical quality materials and devices help run shopping centers, Amazon warehouses, commerce, and shipping.

Clearly, you can see how one invention continues to propel other new inventions due to societal need at certain times in history. This is how innovation and capitalism work hand in hand. Without a need or want and profit motive, there is no innovation; and without innovation we would have no businesses for capitalism to prosper.[11]

References

1. *Criteria for Accrediting Engineering Programs, 2016 – 2017.* Accreditation Board for Engineering and Technology, Inc. 2017. URL: `https://www.abet.org/accreditation/accreditation-criteria/criteria-for-accrediting-engineering-programs-2016-2017/#definitions` (cited on page 147).
2. OECD. *Frascati Manual 2015.* 2015, page 400. DOI: `https://doi.org/https://doi.org/10.1787/9789264239012-en`. URL: `https://www.oecd-ilibrary.org/content/publication/9789264239012-en` (cited on pages 147, 148).
3. Steven D Peterson, Peter E Jaret, and Barbara Findlay Schenck. *Enhance Your Business Plan with Research and Development.* URL: `https://www.dummies.com/business/start-a-business/business-plans/enhance-your-business-plan-with-research-and-development/` (cited on page 149).
4. Daniel A Tysver. *WHY PROTECT SOFTWARE THROUGH PATENTS?* 2018. URL: `https://www.bitlaw.com/software-patent/why-patent.html` (cited on page 150).
5. Scott Gamble. *How to Run R&D Like a Business.* June 2010. URL: `http://viewpoints.io/entry/how-to-run-rd-like-a-business` (cited on page 150).

6. *2018 Global Innovation 1000: What the Top Innovators Get Right*. Strategy&, PricewaterhouseCoopers. Oct. 2018. URL: https://www.strategyand.pwc.com/media/file/2018-Global-Innovation-1000-Fact-Pack.pdf (cited on page 150).

7. Martin. *Research and Development (R&D) | Overview & Process*. July 2014. URL: https://www.cleverism.com/rd-research-and-development-overview-process/ (cited on page 151).

8. Barry Jaruzelski and Cesare R Mainardi. *The World's 10 Most Innovative Companies, And How They Do It*. Apr. 2011. URL: http://www.forbes.com/2011/04/04/10-top-innovative-companies-apple-google-leadership-managing-how.html (cited on page 151).

9. Raymond M Wolfe. *Business R&D Performed in the United States Reached $356 Billion in 2015*. Aug. 2017. URL: http://www.nsf.gov/statistics/2017/nsf17320/ (cited on page 151).

10. *Rates of return to investment in science and innovation*. type. London: Frontier Economics Ltd., July 2014. URL: https://assets.publishing.service.gov.uk/government/uploads/system/uploads/attachment_data/file/333006/bis-14-990-rates-of-return-to-investment-in-science-and-innovation-revised-final-report.pdf (cited on page 151).

11. James Fallows. *The 50 Greatest Breakthroughs Since the Wheel*. Nov. 2013. URL: http://www.theatlantic.com/magazine/archive/2013/11/innovations-list/309536 (cited on page 152).

VIII

Is Now The Opportunity To Build Your Patent Portfolio?

Overview of Patents

A *patent*: According to the United States Patent and Trademark Office, a *patent* is explained as follows:

> A patent is a type of property right. It gives the patent holder the right, for a limited time, to exclude others from making, using, offering to sell, selling, or importing into the United States the subject matter that is within the scope of protection granted by the patent. The USPTO determines whether a patent should be granted in a particular case. However, it is up to the patent holder to enforce his or her own rights if the USPTO does grant a patent.[1]

A patent is a valuable business asset to own, but only when a patent is appropriate. Some companies are built on their patent library; others merely use trade secrets. IBM has the most patents with over 100,000 and counting; over 9,000 in 2017 alone and almost double its closest competition, which is Samsung with over 8,000.[2,3]

A famous company that chooses to use trade secrets is Coca-Cola. They keep their secret ingredient in a SunTrust bank vault in Atlanta, Georgia. You might be surprised to find out that most inventions are not patented. According to research from the University of Lisbon Economics Department, investigation into patent records indicate "a relative low number of important innovations are patented" with patent propensity varying across industrial sectors and type of organization with about 10% of *important* inventions being patented.[4] "This implies that most important innovations are not patented. For most innovations, the innovating companies rely on trade secrecy, lead time/first to market advantages, or other strategies, instead of on the patent system."[5] For the other inventions that could be patented, "devising a patent portfolio development strategy early on can be a wise investment to help the company develop and build a strong foundational asset on which to grow. This investment will likely reward the company with positive returns for years to come. The focus should be on building a high-quality patent portfolio and not file everything."[6]

Four Types of Intellectual Property

Smart companies figure out how to get processes done faster, cheaper, with fewer snags, less rework, less waste, etc. Smart companies figure out what their customers want next, and give it to them. So, smart companies rise above their competition by out-thinking them. Often, a very valuable asset and reason for a smart company's success is due to the intellectual property (IP, valuable creations) that a company amasses. You need to be able to protect your valuable asset, and the approach you use depends on which type of IP you are protecting. There are four important categories of IP.

1. IP can concern a product.

IP can concern a product (such as Apple's iPhone) or a feature (such as the unusual shape of a bottle of Coca Cola). The product or feature may be due to the efforts of a single person, a group, or even an organization. These types of IP can be protected with a patent.

2. IP can consist of something that a person has authored.

IP can consist of something that a person has authored such as a book, a movie, music, or artwork. Again, the work may originate from one person, a group, or an organization. This type of IP can be protected via copyrighting.

3. Your brand name itself is valuable.

You do NOT want a competitor using your firm's name (or a confusingly similar name: Will-Mart, Tako Bell, Furd Motors, etc.). In particular, you don't want competitors selling their inferior goods and services masquerading as yours. So, to protect yourself, you can trademark your firm's name and your firm's products and services. There is an interesting case involving mayonnaise. Hellman's has trademark protected two brands of mayonnaise, which are essentially identical, called Hellman's and Best Foods. Hellman's mayonnaise is only sold east of the Rocky Mountains (i.e., the Dakotas, Nebraska, Kansas, Oklahoma, and Texas and all states eastward). Best Food's mayonnaise is sold west of the Rocky Mountains. Why the two brand names? When Hellman's bought the company that owned Best Food's mayonnaise, by that time, Best Foods had such a strong market presence and reputation that the decision was made to leave well enough alone and keep the two brand names separately trademarked and separated geographically.

4. Trade secret valuable products or processes.

You may have a product or process that is so important for your firm that you fear that any public disclosure (such as by applying for a patent) would reveal too much to competitors. The way against this is to keep it a secret, a trade secret. But, to do so requires that strict secrecy is enforced—any disclosure and it's gone forever. Famous examples of trade secrets include the search algorithm that Google uses, the formula for Listerine mouthwash, the process the New York Times uses to amass its influential list of best-selling book, and the formula for WD-40, the multipurpose lubricant (it got its name from being the 40th attempt to create a water dispersing agent).

Patent Planning

Most people think you can or should patent everything. Although patenting has its advantages, it may not align with your business model as 90% of inventions are NOT patented. When deciding whether to patent a product, it must be determined if it is even patentable. Some items are not patentable under the United States Patent and Trademark Office (USPTO) definition. Some products and processes are not patentable because someone else has the patent. Some products are better off not patented, but treated as a trade secret. Even if your product is patentable and better patented than trade secreted, you should do a cost-benefit analysis. The patent process is very expensive.

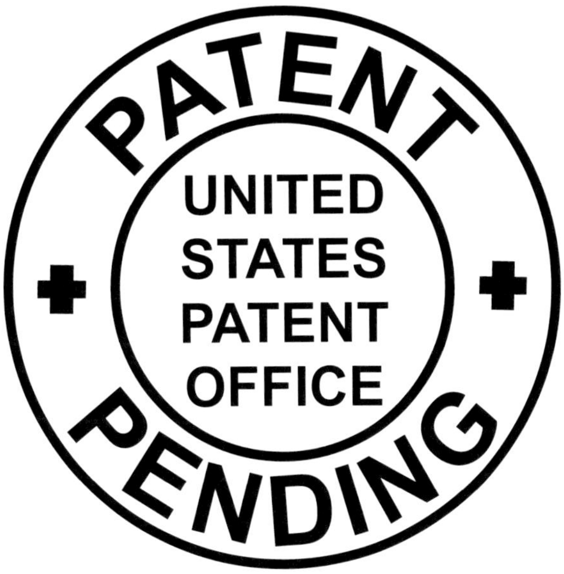

Applications, legal fees, searching for violations of your patent, and subsequent patent prosecution are all very costly, and it might not be worth the expense to patent a product. If you decide that the patent process is worth the expense and time to execute, there are many things to know about how a patent works ahead of time.[7]

Patents help protect products and processes. Patents should not be confused with copyrights and trademarks. Copyrights protect music, art, slogans, poems, and books (such as the one you are currently reading). Trademarks help protect a name or a logo, or a logo attached to a name. If you are seeking any one of these types of intellectual property or its protection, you should see an IP attorney. There are two types of patents: a utility patent and a design patent. "In general terms, a utility patent protects the way an article is used and works (**35 U.S.C. 101**).[8] while a design patent protects the way an article looks (**35 U.S.C. 171**).[9] The ornamental appearance for an article includes its shape/configuration or surface ornamentation applied to the article, or both.

Both *design* and *utility patents* may be obtained on an article if invention resides both in its utility and ornamental appearance. Once the patent is applied for, it enters the patent application process and is examined by a patent examiner for approval or denial. Once approved, you must pay maintenance fees, otherwise the patent expires. It is also important to make sure your patent is filed and registered in the appropriate countries where you are seeking patent protection.[10]

Patent Portfolio

If a business decides to patent and build a *patent portfolio*, the business must have a well thought out and developed comprehensive strategy. When building a successful patent portfolio, consider the application, processing, prosecution, annual maintenance, potential defense, and multiple country jurisdiction fees. Do a cost-benefit analysis. When will the patents start to pay off? Are these intellectual property assets for sole use by the business, or will the business be selling or licensing the invention for fees or royalties? These are important questions since it must be determined if the patent assets are self-sustaining, profitable, or result in negative net revenues. If a patent operates at a loss, then for how long? Will it ever be money generating or profitable?

From a business standpoint, patents could be essential to a competitive advantage for a number of years; however, without a patent, the product would be worthless. The perfect example of seeking a competitive advantage through a patent is a pharmaceutical product. After pouring millions of dollars into research and development (R&D), the company must protect the product and itself through a patent for competitive advantage. If the drug is not patent protected, the competition will *reverse engineer* the ingredients and release it on the market to compete with your heavily invested product. The patent is the legal way to protect your hard work and large investments in order to receive your return on investment and a fair profit. In the case of pharmaceuticals, drugs receive patent protection in the US for twenty years. Therefore, it must be the strategy of the drug company to maximize the most revenues it can within the twenty-year window before the generic drug is legally able to be released into general competition. As you can see, the pharmaceutical company has an objective that aligns with its business goals, as your business should too. You must be well aware of your short and long-term business objectives and goals when it involves patent strategy. A part of the patent strategy is to have a patent budget. This patent budget should be a separate line item, not merely part of legal fee line item.

On one hand, with respect to company patent goals, you can invent, secure a patent, then sue for infringement when companies or businesses encroach on your patent for retroactive and future licensing fees. On the other hand, you can be the company that could be sued for using a device or technology by that type of company who invents, patents, then lies in wait to collect its royalties from unsuspecting innocent end-user victims. When you get into the patent game, be aware of these and other shady type of loopholes. Without further ado, here are inventions you may think are patent-free but could get you sued:[11]

- Magic Missiles on Dungeons and Dragons
- Internet Routers in Local Coffee Shops
- Podcasting, Office Scanners, iPhone Apps
- Publishing Messages Online, SSL Encryption, 3-D Printing

In certain instances, you must patent to be rewarded and patent to be protected from lawsuits.

The following is a list of those inventions that were never patented, or patented and not maintained resulting in expiration and the inventor made NO money:[12]

- World Wide Web - Tim Berners Lee
- Ballpoint Pen - Laszio Biro
- AK-47 - Mikhail Kalashnikov
- Karaoke Machine - Daisuke Inoue
- Computer Mouse - Douglas Engelbart

- Magnetic Credit Card Strip – Ron Klein
- Matches- John Walker
- Tetris- Alexey Pajitnov
- Emoticon - Harvey Ball

In certain instances, you must patent to be rewarded and patent to be protected from lawsuits. Patents can work both ways, so be vigilant when intellectual property rights could be involved.

As with everything in business, plan early. Patent, trademark, and copyright planning should start at the time the business plan is written and the start of your company. When this is done, availability, protection, naming, branding, patent protection, copyright protection, trademark protection and planning all fall into place. Ask yourself some questions. How will the business name, product and product name, packaging, slogan and logo be distributed and marketed:

- With investors, partners, manufacturers, distributors and retailers
- In print
- On television and radio
- On the web
- With search engine optimization
- On social media
- And will it be unique enough to differentiate from your competition?

When intellectual property is planned for early and properly, there will be more opportunity for your business in your marketplace.[13]

Technology Transfer

A major opportunity for patent business involves *technology transfer*. When transferring technology, patent strategy plays a vital role. Tech transfer involves the sharing of technologies between public and private entities for commercialization of a patent or invention. Technology transfer with universities and government agencies can be very lucrative and provide many new business opportunities. Public and private partnerships are becoming more common, and require careful negotiations and the understanding of state and federal regulations.

Specifically, patent issues and ownership could be called into question and have major implications on the viability of the venture. As a private business you want to avoid costly litigation with a government, since governments will have many more legal resources than you. For this reason, there are organizations that exist to help promote these tech transfer ventures by helping to lessen the potential risk of the parties involved. For example, the American Association of Universities is a not for profit organization representing universities and their technology transfer interests.

> "Technology transfer is the process that universities and other research organizations use to translate research discoveries and scientific findings into new products, technologies, drugs and other services that benefit the public. AAU promotes activities to improve university technology transfer through providing a forum through which its members share information about institutional policies and best practices they use to move ideas from the laboratory to the marketplace. AAU also advocates for maintaining and strengthening federal technology transfer policies, including the Bayh-Dole Act of 1980 which fundamentally changed the

> nation's system of technology transfer by enabling universities to retain title to inventions and take the lead in patenting and licensing groundbreaking discoveries. Universities and medical schools rely on a robust, equitable patent system to ensure research discoveries can be transferred to businesses that can develop them into marketable products that improve our quality of life and fuel the economy. This measure would help ensure the strength of this technology transfer process, which contributes significantly to our nation's leadership in science and technology. We look forward to continuing to work with Congress, as well as with USPTO Director Andrei Iancu, toward our shared goals of curtailing abusive patent litigation and reinforcing the strength of the U.S. patent system."[14]

Other not for profit membership organizations such as the "Alliance of Technology Transfer Professionals" [†] are also available, with all parties looking to be fairly represented at the deal making table by lobbying for favorable legislation. If your business does decide to venture into tech transfer agreements, it would be advisable to look into the legal and patent ramifications, as well as joining one of these organizations that best suit your needs.

Major Takeaway

Patent decisions must be taken very seriously, and a patent attorney must be consulted immediately once a patent is contemplated and as you are inventing. Timing can be everything and you do not want to disclose your idea to the wrong people.

When contemplating a patent, it is important to understand the "risks" associated with taking an invention to market. The number one risk is protection. A Patent Attorney will best understand the process in order to correctly drat the patent application, providing the best protection and less risk of denial, narrowness, or obsolescence. Mitigating risk and gaining the most patent protections is the foundation of building a strong, valuable, and effective patent portfolio.

The ability for the patent attorney to implement a strategy for the product or technology to meet the companies business plan and business model are vital to success in domestic and/or international export markets. Starting with a competent patent attorney will mitigate risks, keep costs under control, provide the best path, and strategies for the highest return on investment.

> "Companies should first consult with the patent attorney to understand the various risks associated in the process of taking an invention to a marketable technology or product. A patent attorney will be able to draft a patent application that is able to give the best protection to the invention, which is the foundation of building an effective patent portfolio. Coherent strategy will effectively link the patent strategy with the strategic needs of the key products of the business that are sold in the domestic or export markets. This will prevent patent costs from spiraling out of control. Every cost must be seen in the context of the likely return on investment, and the risks involved in the process of taking an invention to a marketable technology or product."[6]

[†]Learn more about the Alliance of Technology Transfer Professionals at: `https://attp.info/learn-about-attp/`

As was mentioned, within the umbrella of protected intellectual property are patents, trademarks, and copyrights. Do everything legally necessary to protect your business' reputation and good name under these intellectual property protection mechanisms.

Case Study

One of our clients was fraudulently induced into purchasing products and services that were held out as a "factory authorized facility" with "trained authorized service technicians." However, when the product did not operate according to the manufacturer's standards, we investigated for our client and we were able to prove to the third-party payer, who made payments on behalf of our client to the fraudulent outfit, was advertising their facility, products, and services with credentials that never existed. We pursued the fraudulent company and its third-party payer, and received a full refund for our client. During the process, to protect its valuable brand, the authentic manufacturer of the product and owner of the brand sent a cease and desist order to the fraudulent firm, and they immediately changed their advertising misrepresentations.

References

1. United States Patent and Trademark Office - An Agency of the Department of Commerce. *Non-provisional (Utility) Patent Application Filing Guide*. Jan. 2014. URL: https://www.uspto.gov/patents-getting-started/patent-basics/types-patent-applications/nonprovisional-utility-patent (cited on page 157).
2. *Patents and Innovation - IBM Research - US*. URL: http://www.research.ibm.com/patents (cited on page 157).
3. *2017 Top 50 US Patent Assignees*. Jan. 2018. URL: https://www.ificlaims.com/rankings-top-50-2017.htm (cited on page 157).
4. Roberto Fontana et al. "Reassessing patent propensity: Evidence from a dataset of R&D awards, 1977–2004". In: *Research Policy* 42.10 (2013). Economics, innovation and history: Perspectives in honour of Nick von Tunzelmann, pages 1780–1792. ISSN: 0048-7333. DOI: https://doi.org/10.1016/j.respol.2012.05.014. URL: http://www.sciencedirect.com/science/article/pii/S0048733313001558 (cited on page 157).
5. Stephan Kinsella. "Study: Most Important Innovations Are Not Patented". In: *Center for the Study of Innovative Freedom* (Nov. 2013). URL: http://c4sif.org/2013/11/study-most-important-innovations-are-not-patented/ (cited on page 157).
6. Lim Hui Yi. "Developing an effective patent portfolio strategy". In: *ATMD Bird & Bird, LLP* (July 2010), pages 2–3. URL: https://s3.amazonaws.com/documents.lexology.com/cc28e785-9846-422c-9955-6f7198f53b61.pdf (cited on pages 157, 162).

7. Lauren Flick. "Inventor alert: Patents aren't all they're built up to be". In: *CNBC* (Sept. 2015). URL: https://www.cnbc.com/2015/09/16/the-case-against-patenting-your-brilliant-invention.html (cited on page 159).

8. United States Code Title 35 §101. Patents. *Inventions patentable* (cited on page 159).

9. United States Code Title 35 §171. Patents. *Patents for designs.* (Cited on page 159).

10. "Patent process overview". In: *United States Patent and Trademark Office* (Nov. 2014). URL: https://www.uspto.gov/patents-getting-started/patent-process-overview (cited on page 159).

11. Dana Liebelson. "8 inventions you thought were patent-free but could get you sued if you use them". In: *Mother Jones* (Nov. 2013). URL: https://www.motherjones.com/politics/2013/11/8-patent-invention-claims/ (cited on page 160).

12. Jessica Best. "10 inventors who never made money from their creations". In: (Oct. 2013). URL: https://www.mirror.co.uk/news/top-tens/10-inventors-who-never-made-2646656 (cited on page 160).

13. Caron Beesley. "How to Choose, Claim, and Protect Your Business Name – Online and Offline". In: (Sept. 2016). URL: http://www.sba.gov/blogs/how-choose-claim-and-protect-your-business-name-online-and-offline (cited on page 161).

14. *Technology Transfer*. URL: https://www.aau.edu/issues/technology-transfer (cited on page 162).

XIX Time To Sell My Business?

Selling

Is now the opportunity to sell my business? Maybe, but what does *sell* actually mean?

According to the Merriam-Webster Dictionary: to *sell*, *sold*, or *selling* is:

1. To transfer (goods) to or render (services) for another in exchange for money; dispose of to a purchaser for a price.
2. To deal in; keep or offer for sale.
3. To make a sale or offer for sale to.

It could always be the opportunity to sell your business. Always ask yourself, what price would I accept to part with or sell my business? You are not going to be involved in your business forever. So, when do you want to exit? Is it a fixed date (such as your 65th birthday)? Is it whenever your business achieves a certain level of success (e.g., it hits target sales, profits, number of employees, or goes national or international)? When your children definitely state that they want nothing to do with your business? Or, is it when you are cash-strapped, worn out, on the brink of bankruptcy, or otherwise have your back to the wall? Rather than being forced to sell, far better to identify some positive triggers and act on them when reached.

Let's define the word "sell." In business, "sell" has many meanings and provides the seller and purchaser many options. For example, are you a company stock owner selling all or part of the shares that you own? Are you a sole proprietor selling your business in an all cash transaction at closing, or are you holding a note on the business, and if the note is defaulted, you might get the business back? Do you own an LLC as a member and are you selling the business LLC, or just all or part of the assets of the LLC, or do you merely own a holding company that owns many separate entities?

As you can see, *sell* has many connotations and options. The best example of choices for a seller and buyer during a buy/sell transaction is when there are separate components that could operate independently of each other if they were sold separately. Imagine an LLC manufacturer named "A," which is owned by two individuals and is a sole member of a retail company named "B," also owning the tradename "C." "A" manufactures, wholesales, distributes, and sells its products retail on-line and wholesales to "B" and other companies. "B" is only a retailer of products sold to it by "A." In addition, the tradename "C" is a dba (doing business as) of "A", only selling "A's" products online and at special events.

This set-up is done for accounting, tax, and legal reasons that best benefit the entire operation

owned by two business partners. It is important to understand that there are multiple entities and sale possibilities.

- All entities may be sold
- Any combination of entities may be sold
- Just one entity may be sold to one or multiple buyers.

These separate parts or entities, if sold separately to different buyers, would either be worth more or less than the sum of the parts. Buyer offers and sale prices could vary dramatically depending on the needs and wants of potential buyers.

Now that you looked at "sell" possibilities, what is your end game? Part of every business plan must have an "exit strategy." Part of owning a business is being able to sell the business. This "exit strategy" should map out your plans to extricate yourself from the business in the MOST favorable fashion, and most at least sketch the time horizon to exit. The last thing you want to be stuck with is a business that can't be sold, and you must walk away from the business with no sale. Too many people wait too long to try to sell their business, their lease expires with no renewal, or the business becomes obsolete and is now worthless.

Here are some reasons businesses are sold:

- Personal situation (e.g., health), family considerations (e.g., geographical relocation), or divorce may force a cash settlement
- Partner(s) wishing to cash out either from their partnership or the entire business
- Death or disability of an owner or key staff member
- Retirement with no family member to take over
- Change of lifestyle
- Run out of money or credit
- Can't keep up with complexities, technology, or other marketplace changes
- Time to take your profit and "cash out" your equity

Timing is everything when selling a business. You want to sell at the top when revenues and profits are the highest and on the upswing. Plan on selling your company before trouble strikes but while the economic climate is favorable. When considering a timely sale, hire a business broker to maintain confidentiality and anonymity. Potential purchasers must not know the identity of the business until a non-disclosure confidentiality agreement is signed by potential purchasers. Only hiring a business broker will maintain confidentiality and the value of the business. It is an undisputed fact that when word gets out that a business will be sold, its value deceases. A business broker will also help to: identify qualified buyers, assist with purchaser financing, eliminate conflicts of interest, guide favorable tax decisions, and facilitate professional referrals to all parties to expedite the sale. However, when selling to a partner, insider, family member, or friend, a business broker may not be needed. In this instance, you might only want a business appraiser to determine the selling price if the price has not been predetermined or there are significant differences in business value.

Buyers of businesses come in all shapes and sizes. They can be individuals, partnerships, limited liability companies, "C," or "S" corporations. These buyers could seek a simple all cash transaction, installments, owner financing, stock swaps, or merger. Realizing the many varieties of buyers and their offers, it is essential to seek counsel from a lawyer, accountant, and business consultant. As a seller, you don't want to be left with the short end of the stick. Issues that must be addressed include limiting liability, taxes, recourse, and future legal action. A qualified team of professionals should limit your exposure to these unwanted and costly post-sale experiences. It is a good idea to invest the money for good counsel, knowledge and expertise upfront than get hit with surprises, lawsuits, and taken to the cleaners after the transaction.

Preparing for a Sale

Prepare well in advance for a sale by steadily increasing revenues and keeping good records. About one to two years before you put the business on the market for sale:

- Prepare professional looking and accurate financial records, balance sheet, profit & loss statement, list of assets and liabilities, and current year tax filing
- Remove poorly performing products from inventory and solidify business structure and customer base
- Terminate all insider transactions
- Eliminate excessive costs and fringe benefits
- Pay all taxes and pay off all debt, if possible
- Prepare two-four years of audited financial statements

It is also a good strategy to make a list and create a PowerPoint presentation with photos of all reasons (along with their values) why a buyer would want to buy your business; including, but not limited to:

- High profit margins, increased annual profits, and long-term contracts
- High revenues per hour of operation
- List of ALL inventory, equipment, material, supplies, and product assets included with the sale
- Ownership of good location real property that goes with the sale
- Low market comparable lease cost
- More than two years left on any renewable lease
- Uniqueness of products, favorable distribution channels, and lack of market competition
- Valuable tradenames, trade dress, trade secrets, patents, and other proprietary processes and any other intellectual property
- Valuable brands, labels, and signage
- Valuable goodwill, strong repeat customer base, industry network, and account history
- Great cash flow, consistent income stream, and life style expense benefits
- Domination of market
- Business model description summary, business plan, and operating manuals
- Demonstrate that all essential equipment is serviced and in good operating order
- Complete turn-key operation with room for growth and expansion
- The ability to employ family members and mix business with pleasure should be stated and accounted for, if applicable
- If advantageous, disclose your reason for selling

It is a good practice to hire a business appraiser for an explanation of the business' worth and market valuation to determine the asking or listing price for the business. You do not want to scare prospective buyers away with too high of an asking price, and you don't want to "give the business away" by listing the sale price too low. During the process of selling a business, it is a good idea to:

- Line up multiple back up buyers, contingent upon a sale falling through
- Keep all lines of communication open with buyers and contingent buyers
- Pre-qualify your potential buyers at or before the time that a non-disclosure is signed
- Request a bank letter of assets or pre-approved financing for the transaction that will meet your terms

- Be prepared to negotiate on the price that has been appraised for reasonable present and future business value
- Document all agreements in writing
  - All potential buyers should sign a nondisclosure/confidentiality agreement before you release any proprietary information in order to protect your business and the business of a future buyer
- Have the signed purchase agreement with multiple non-refundable deposits placed into escrow as the sale proceeds and any contingencies are met
- State conditions, which if met, would enable releases from the escrow account
- If there is a lease, have the new buyer meet the landlord to have the documents drafted and signed to add the buyer to the lease. Then, remove the seller from the lease, contingent on the sale closing with renewal lease for the buyer, if necessary, and agreed upon in the contract of sale
- Be ready to sign a covenant not to compete with the new buyers within a certain distance radius and period of time
- Meet with your lawyer, accountant, and business consultant before, during, and after the sale to fully take advantage of all the favorable business, legal, and tax decisions that will need to be made

Sales and sale prices of small businesses are on an upswing. In 2012, 4,730 small businesses, at an average sale price of 164,000, were sold. In 2015, 7,222 small businesses, at an average sale price of $199,000, were sold. Of the businesses sold, "Restaurants accounted for 22% of all business sales in 2015, the highest of any industry," and the internet Business-to-Business (B2B) industry had the highest average sale price of $364,000.[1] These are the types of statistics and information that you should look at when considering selling your business in order to determine industry and economy valuation. If you want your business to be one of those sold, now is the time to start planning for your best opportunity to sell your business, at the highest sale price.

Takeaway Lesson

"Selling" a business is one of the most important parts of owning a business. Therefore, always maintain your business as ready to sell. You never know when an unsolicited "offer you can't refuse" will come along. The main advantage and the windfall of profits can be at the time of the sale of the business. Over the years, you have invested money, time, resources, and equity into the business. Selling is the time to reap those rewards and parlay the sales proceeds into a new venture with more potential, diversify your investments, and/or retirement.

Here are examples of successful business sales that came along unsolicited, but the owners had planned for and were ready to sell due to a smart business model and plan, readiness, and timing:

"Sekindo, MyRoll and Dollar Shave Club are merely reflections of good ideas backed by dedication, combined with good timing, which ultimately allowed their business plans to ride the wave of success."[2] These were sold for huge paydays in the tens or hundreds of millions of dollars.

Our consulting firm was involved in a sale of a business that had an exit strategy and was listed for sale for 6 months before it sold. Compare our sale to what happens when "the exit strategy" is not good or not part of a business plan. Our consulting firm was involved in a sale of a business that was listed for sale for 6 months and took 60 days to close. The business was in existence

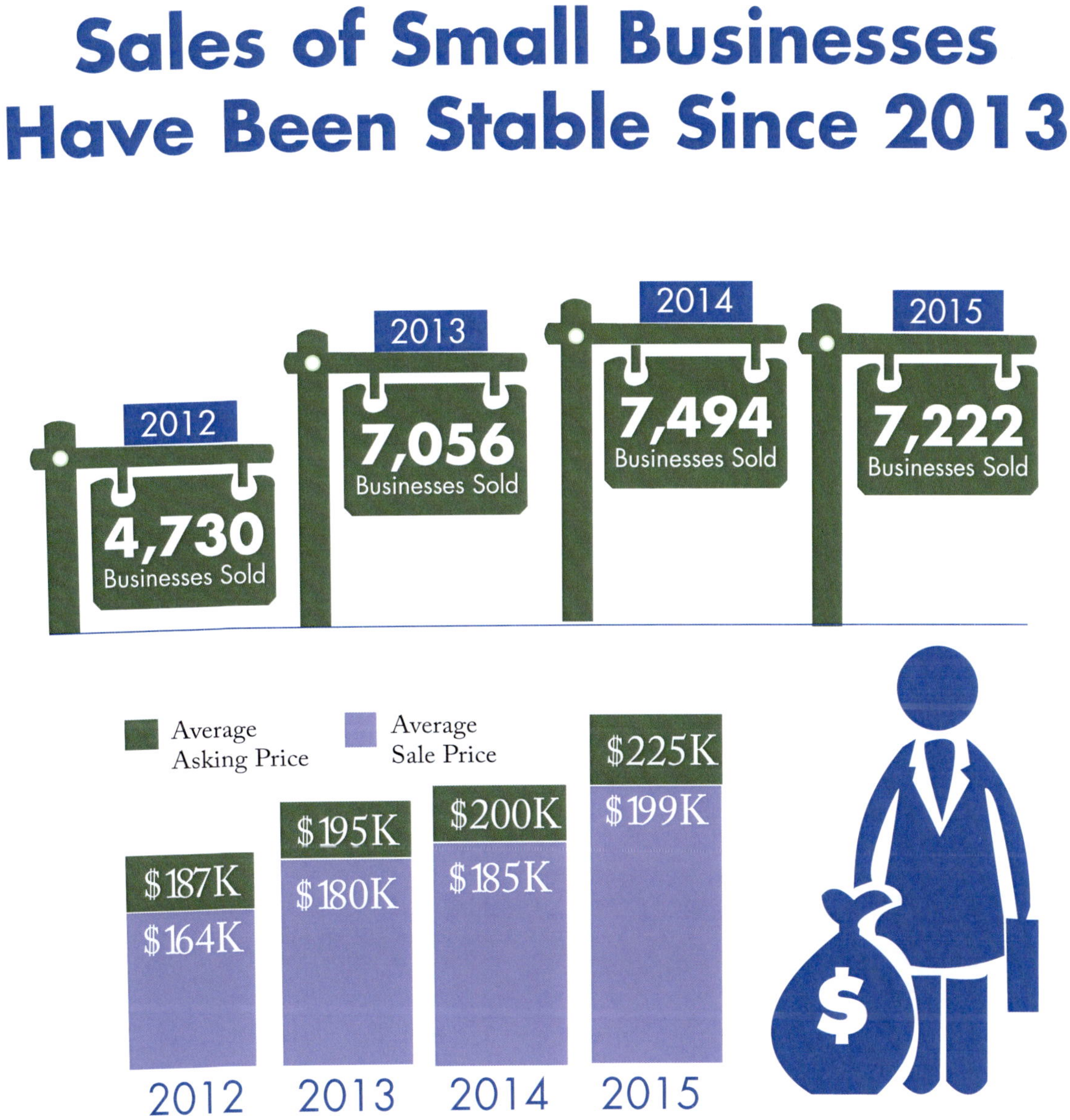

Infographic depicting sales and sale prices of small business rising.[1]

for 9 years, and we did everything stated in this chapter to sell the company. We sold the entire vertically integrated small business with three profit centers for 7 times annual profit. We were able to demonstrate perceived value and show future earnings estimates, such that the purchaser understood the greater earnings potential and was willing to pay for it.

Here is an example of an unsolicited sale and a very bad deal prompted by a partner who wanted out for all the wrong reasons. However, it was a great deal for the two partners who stayed!

> "Swiftkey was created by three friends (all Cambridge graduates) – Chris Hill-Scott, Jon Reynolds and Ben Medlock – in 2008. The app uses artificial intelligence to predict what smartphone users will type next and was recently purchased by Microsoft for a reported £170m. Unfortunately, only two of the three founders cashed in on the deal. Hill-Scott became disillusioned with the startup lifestyle early on and decided to get rid of his shares and take a job with the civil service instead. How much did he get for his stake in a company that would go on to be one of the most successful UK tech start-ups of recent times? Hill-Scott swapped his shares to his friends in exchange for a bicycle. Yes, a push bike. Reynolds and Medlock both made a reported £25 million each from the sale to Microsoft, and Hill-Scott tweeted that it was the greatest mistake of his life."[3]

References

1. "Infographic: It's a Great Time for Buying or Selling a Business". In: *SCORE* (Feb. 2016). URL: https://www.score.org/resource/infographic-it%E2%80%99s-great-time-buying-or-selling-business (cited on pages 170, 171).
2. Yoav Vilner. "3 Stories Of Smaller Companies Bought By A Major Name". In: *Inc.com* (Jan. 2017). URL: http://www.inc.com/yoav-vilner/3-stories-of-smaller-companies-bought-by-a-major-name.html (cited on page 170).
3. Peter Flanagan. "Some of the worst business deals ever made". In: (June 2017). URL: http://www.thinkbusiness.ie/articles/bad-business-ideas (cited on page 172).

X

Endnote: Learning To Think Opportunistically

Introduction

What makes some business people incredibly successful while others bang away at endless mediocrity has been explained in a variety of ways. Some simply cite "luck" as the deciding factor—per the billionaire J. Paul Getty, the three rules to follow to be rich are simply (1) rise early, (2) work hard, and (3) strike oil.

Others attribute grit. For example, it is said that Thomas Edison, in trying to invent an electric light bulb, went through 1,000 designs before he found one that worked. When asked about the many failures, he said they were not failures, he learned from each one what didn't work, and that was progress.

We offer a different explanation as to why Jeff Bezos has succeeded with Amazon, Elon Musk with Tesla, Howard Schultz with Starbucks, Richard Branson with the Virgin Group, among many, many others—they each learned to look at the world opportunistically. They saw new uses for technology, they envisioned the need for a "third space" beyond the personal and the public, and they were not afraid to pursue their perceived opportunity and to do so optimistically. As Henry Ford once said, whether you think you can or think you can't, you're right.

Keys to Identifying and Acting on Opportunity

We believe there are three keys to successfully identifying and taking advantage of opportunities that come your way: be optimistic, re-frame situations positively, and constantly ask questions. Understanding these practices and actually doing them will increase your odds of success, both personal and professional.

Optimism

One of the key ingredients to thinking opportunistically is to be optimistic. Be upbeat, and continuously believe that good things are about to happen to you. When you can visualize rather specifically what good things are about to happen, they will. There is a relatively new field of psychology called positive psychology. Scientists practicing in that field study what makes some people happy and how to sustain that happiness. They have also found the following: happy people (compared to those what are significantly less happy) tend to rise to leadership positions, to live longer, to experience fewer illnesses, to recover more quickly from diseases, to earn more on the job, to take fewer sick days, to have more friends, to get promoted higher and faster, and to enjoy life more. While this is not the book to explain how to be happier, there are a couple of steps you should take.

At the end of each day, review it and assess it on a scale of 1 to 10. A "1" is the worst day of your life; a "10" is the best day of your life. A "5" is an average day, while a "3" is a poor day and a "7" is a good day. For each day, what happened that caused you to give it the score that you did? What could you have done differently to get a higher score? What will you do tomorrow to get a higher score?

Also at the end of the day, discover what you are grateful for that day. Perhaps it is the unexpected and stunning beauty of a sunrise, perhaps it is a surprise compliment from a person whom you admire, perhaps it is the satisfaction of having done something that you are proud of (you had a novel idea, a plan that worked out to your advantage, there was a brilliant action by a person you had a lot of faith in, you surprised yourself by your creativity, etc.), perhaps it is something you learned that holds great promise for you, or perhaps it is something else. Whatever it is, write it down and think about it. If your gratitude is due to a person (a loved one, a friend, a business associate, an employee, a teacher, a religious leader, a politician, etc.), write a letter to that person explaining your reasons for gratitude and sincerely thanking that person. If you want two people to have a day that is a "10," send that letter to that person.

Vigorous exercise has several benefits for you, not the least of which is that exercise releases dopamine in your brain which leads to positive feelings. So, if you are feeling blue, or stymied by a problem, take a hike. 20-30 minutes is about the right amount of time for a session of exercise in order to start feeling better. Many people get their best ideas when they are on a bicycle, swimming in a pool, or on a treadmill. Get moving!

Finally, learn something about yourself. Where are you happiest—at the beach, on a mountain, in a museum, at a shopping mall, a quiet evening at home, or where else? Who are you with when you are happiest? What are you doing when you are happiest—visiting a new destination, enjoying new cuisine, at sea on a cruise, etc.? Try to envision and recreate occasions when you are at your peak. Don't let life be a set of random occurrences—figure out what makes you happy and try to engineer those circumstances.

Reframing Situations

If you have ever been cut from a sports team, received a poor grade in a school assignment or course, or been fired from a job, it is all to easy to feel negatively about yourself. In each of those three cases you might say to yourself, "I'm untalented, I'm stupid, or I'll never be successful." Those are all negative characterizations of those situations. Positive views of each situation are quite different: "Well, I'm not gifted at that sport, so I'll go look for another one that I am more fit for." "I just don't seem to get subject matter X, so I'll change my major to one where I get higher grades in that subject matter." "My skills really didn't fit that company's needs, so I must do a better job of finding a company that can use my unique set of skills."

It is a bit like the old situation of "is the glass half empty or half full." The correct answer is that it is neither, until you have made up your mind which it is. YOU get to decide if your life is all roses and sunshine, or rocks and gloom. The story is told of the 12-year-old daughter who pestered her parents over several years for her own horse. Her parents didn't want the bother or the expense of a horse, so they cruelly laid out a large mound of horse manure on the living room rug on her birthday morning. When the girl came downstairs, she squealed with delight, and started digging through the pile of horse manure. Her parents, stunned by her reactions and actions, asked her, "What are you doing?" The excited girl said, "With all this manure, there must me a horse in here somewhere."

In general, you want to take disappointments and turn them around. You want to go from fretting about failure to thinking up new ways to succeed. Focusing upon the past is useful, but only up to the point that you now confidently know how to keep that irritant from happening again.

Constantly Ask Questions

The astute reader will have noted that several of our chapters begin with "Is now the opportunity to or the time to..." You can spend your day worrying about problems (our advice: get someone else to solve them—many issues are beneath you) or your can spend your day thinking up better ways to do business. Each time you encounter a person, ask yourself "ideally, what should this person be doing?" Each time you look at a machine, ask yourself "is there a better way (faster, cheaper, easier) to do this?" Each time you are presented with a situation, you want to ask yourself, "Where is the advantage here for me?" Be pleased with, but don't be content with the status quo. The Japanese espouse the concept of "kaizen," which is the process of making consistent, small improvements all the time. If you can just make a 1% improvement each day, by the end of the year you'll be four times (4x!) better.

You want to walk around the office questioning everything and asking yourself, where's the opportunity here? Each day, you need to come up with at least one new insight, one concept, one approach that has potential payoff for your business. If nothing occurs to you on site, go home and read a business biography (Steve Jobs, Howard Schultz, Warren Buffett, Donald Trump, Richard Branson, Sam Walton, Sheryl Sandberg,...need more suggestions?). In that biography, try to learn what that person did to become so successful—and what are you going to do about it?

Putting It All Together

We all have the same 24 hours each day open to us. You have the same 24 hours as Warren Buffett does, the president of the United States, the Chairman of the Joint Chiefs of Staff, each Nobel Prize winner, each billionaire, each creator of every billion-dollar unicorn, and every low life manager in a giant bureaucracy. How are they spending their allotted 24 hours? Are they out partying and watching the latest and greatest on Netflix? Or are they thinking about ways they could be improving their operations? It's a choice, and it's up to you.

Our preferences, and our suggestions to you, are simple: Look forward to the future with great hope and excitement. Learn from your past failures and disappointments, but don't dwell on them. On those occasions where you find yourself backpedaling into negativism, quickly restructure your thinking so that there is a positive take on the situation that presents itself. Finally, spend your waking minutes asking what is going on and figuring out how the status quo can be improved upon. Frequently pose "what ifs" to your friends and fellow coworkers to learn from them. Make sure you learn at least one new chunk of useful information each day.

We wish you the very best success at finding and exploiting business opportunities, and may they prove incredibly prosperous!

Appendix

Author Curriculum Vitaes

See LinkedIn™ pages for author curriculum vitaes.

Business Management & Consultant Group (BMCG)
`http://www.managerandconsultant.com/`
Francis D. (Doug) Tuggle
`https://www.linkedin.com/in/doug-tuggle-117b01/`
Chad Berl
`https://www.linkedin.com/in/chadberl/`
Seth J. Berl
`https://www.linkedin.com/in/sethberl/`
`http://www.sethberl.com/`
`http://www.consultsmartec.com/`
Lenny Berl
`https://www.linkedin.com/in/lennyberl/`

Index

Index